Physical Characteri
Curly Coated R
(from the The Kennel Club

Body: Well sprung ribs, good depth of brisket, not long in loin or tucked up.

Hindquarters: Strong, muscular, hock low to ground and well bent.

Tail: Moderately short, carried straight, covered with curls, tapering towards point, never gay or curled.

Size: Desirable height at withers: dogs: 69 cms (27 ins); bitches: 64 cms (25 ins).

Coat: Mass of crisp, small curls all over.

Feet: Round, compact, toes well arched.

Curly Coated Retriever

By Phillip Mathis

Discover the origins of this most ancient of retriever breeds, whose origins are submerged in 15th-century Britain. From the likely crosses to German Poodles and the 'Old Water Dog' comes this unique water retriever with tremendous swimming and hunting power. Trace the breed's development from Britain to Australia and New Zealand, where the breed has a significant following, to the US, where the breed is just beginning to establish a stronghold.

Underneath the Curly's unique coat of crisp, tight curls is a dog equally unique—meet the independent and intelligent Curly Coated Retriever. Find out about the breed's personality and trainability as well as its physical characteristics, including the possible hereditary conditions that challenge the Curly's well-being.

Learn the requirements of a well-bred Curly Coated Retriever by studying the description of the breed as set forth in The Kennel Club's breed standard. Both show dogs and pets must possess key characteristics as outlined in the breed standard.

Be advised about choosing a reputable breeder and selecting a healthy, typical puppy. Understand the responsibilities of ownership, including home preparation, acclimatisation, the vet and prevention of common puppy problems.

Enter into a sensible discussion of dietary and feeding considerations, exercise, grooming, travelling and identification of your dog. This chapter discusses Curly Coated Retriever care for all stages of development.

CONTENTS

PUBLISHED IN THE UNITED KINGDOM BY:

INTERPET
PUBLISHING
Vincent Lane, Dorking, Surrey RH4 3YX England

ISBN 1-842860-15-4

PHOTOGRAPHS BY CAROL ANN JOHNSON AND MICHAEL TRAFFORD
with additional photos by Norvia Behling, TJ Calhoun, Carolina Biological Supply, Doskocil, Isabelle Français, James Hayden-Yoav, James R Hayden, RBP, Bill Jonas, Dwight R Kuhn, Dr Dennis Kunkel, Mikki Pet Products, Phototake, Jean Claude Revy, Dr Andrew Spielman and Alice van Kempen.
Illustrations by Reneé Low.

The publisher wishes to thank Audrey Nicholls, Hayden & Gladys Phillips, Nicola Phillips-McFarlane and the rest of the owners of the dogs featured in this book.

Unlike all the other retrieving breeds, the Curly Coated Retriever possesses many unique features, including his hallmark coat and water-dog abilities.

The Curly Coated Retriever is utilised to retrieve game on land and from the water.

The Curly Coated Retriever is considered the most unique of all of the retriever breeds. With his sturdy legs and body covered in a mass of tight, shiny curls, he appears more to be a cuddly teddy bear than a capable and courageous hunting dog. He is also the least recognised of the retrievers and is often mistaken for the Poodle or the Irish Water Spaniel, his distant relatives of centuries ago. Although the Curly is a most popular gundog in New Zealand and Australia, where he is prized for his strength, courage and tenacity, the breed is not well known in countries like the United States or other parts of the world.

ORIGIN AND ESTABLISHMENT OF THE BREED IN ENGLAND

Unlike the histories of the other retriever breeds, few specifics are known about the history and development of the Curly in its native England. However, pre-1800 writings do offer valid evidence of the breed's existence centuries earlier; references dating back to the fifteenth century describe 'sagacious' curly-coated spaniels and water dogs who possessed outstanding hunting and retrieving ability. Author Phillip Ashburton wrote about Curly Coated Retrievers used for hunting around 1490 in Lincolnshire and Norfolk, the land of Robin Hood and his merry band. Centuries later, a reference in the *Sportsmen's Cabinet* in

BRAIN AND BRAWN

Since dogs have been inbred for centuries, their physical and mental characteristics are constantly being changed to suit man's desires for hunting, retrieving, scenting, guarding and warming their masters' laps. During the past 150 years, dogs have been judged according to physical characteristics as well as functional abilities. Few breeds can boast a genuine balance between physique, working ability and temperament.

1803 suggested that the Curly is a descendant of the 'Old Water Dog' with the following: 'These dogs are exceedingly angular in appearance and most probably derived their origin from the Greenland dog blended with some particular race of their own. The hair of these dogs must be adhering to the body in natural elastic curls, not loose or long and shaggy.'

Subsequent documentation from the mid-1800s offers several other accounts of the Curly's place in evolution as a gundog in England. Writer John Scott wrote in 1820 in the *Sportsman's Repository*, 'The original Water Dog of the opposite continent, being long since adopted in this country and in some maritime districts, is still preserved in a state of purity, but the breed is more generally intermixed with the Water Spaniel and Newfoundland Dog.'

Most breed historians assume that the St. John's Newfoundland, the Tweed Water Spaniel, the Irish Water Spaniel and the Poodle may have contributed to the development of the Curly Coated Retriever in England. Because all of these breeds were evolving at about the same time, it is also possible that the reverse is true, and that the Curly is the dominant link behind the development of those other breeds.

Some authorities believe that the Curly Coated Retriever was crossed with the original Poodle of Germany, with the goal of improving the coat and elegance of the Curly and the staying power and sagacity of the Poodle. Others claim that the mere fact that the Curly Coated Retriever is the only breed named for its curly coat is an indication that this was the first of all the curly-coated breeds. Unfortunately, since the hunters and breeders of the mid-1800s did not document their breeding practices or maintain breeding ledgers, there is no written record of breedings or of the people who were involved in the development of today's Curly to prove any of these theories.

The early Curly Coated Retriever was frequently referred to as a 'meat dog,' a generic term referring to a dog that would find and retrieve the birds regardless of hunting conditions or the gentility of his hunting master. Such was his nose and tenacity that the Curly was often used to find and retrieve birds left in a field already covered by 'other breeds' during a driven shoot. Such a dog was an invaluable aid to the common man who hunted birds in order to provide meat for his family's dinner table.

In 1837, Thomas Bell wrote of the Curly in the *British Quadrupeds*: 'The peculiar qualities and propensities of this dog, its exquisite sense of smell, its sagacity, strength and aquatic habits, have rendered it a most useful and important servant to a particular class of persons of the North of England and Scotland who live principally by shooting waterfowl, in the retrieving of which these dogs exhibit the highest degree of docility and hardihood.' These remarks seem to validate the 'meat-dog' Curly and the class of people most inclined to own and utilise the dog for bird work in water and afield.

Despite his murky history, there is definite proof that the Curly Coated Retriever was the first breed to be classified by The Kennel Club as a retriever and was the first retriever to be exhibited in England as a show dog, the latter occurring in 1860. Four years later, The Kennel Club split retrievers into two classes: Retrievers—Curly Coated and Retrievers—Wavy Coated, offering

GENUS *CANIS*
Dogs and wolves are members of the genus *Canis*. Wolves are known scientifically as *Canis lupus* while dogs are known as *Canis domesticus*. Dogs and wolves are known to interbreed. The term *canine* derives from the Latin derived word *Canis*. The term 'dog' has no scientific basis but has been used for thousands of years. The origin of the word 'dog' has never been authoritatively ascertained.

the Curly official recognition as its own breed. The Curly continued to be shown on the bench but, by the late 1800s, the Labrador and the Flat Coated Retriever far outnumbered Curlies at the shows. The Curly's popularity waned as the public showed a decided preference for the other retriever breeds.

As happened with most other large breeds, the two World Wars decimated breed numbers and in 1919 only five Curlies were registered with The Kennel Club. The road back was long and slow, and after a brief surge in popularity during the late 1930s, numbers plummeted again, with only 13 registered in 1942 and

Despite the breed's small numbers, the Curly has had some spectacular moments in the show ring.

1943. The next few years were still lean, but a bit more promising, with 90 registrations by 1947.

As there were so few Curly breeders during the early 1900s, the few predominant kennel prefixes of that time can be found in most Curly pedigrees if they were to be traced back many generations. Names most commonly known were those of Preston, Penworthan, Knysna, Notlaw and Coombehurst.

By the early 1930s, the Darelyn and Snaphill Curly kennels were producing noteworthy Curlies, but their progress was interrupted by the Second World War. Darelyn, however, resurrected during the 1940s with their foundation stock, Delilah of Darelyn and Dru of Darelyn. Their progeny continued into the 1950s, along with those of the Akrow Kennels, who gave us the important Turkamann and Sorona stock during that decade.

The Curly finally gained real prominence during the 1950s and 1960s, and breeders in Australia,

A long-lived, active dog, the Curly Coated Retriever is the choice of discriminating dog folk seeking a highly trainable, responsive companion. This 11-year-old veteran is still working.

New Zealand and the United States began to import Curly breeding stock from England. Darelyn Aristocrat, Irishit Straight Line and Prince of Knocksginan were imported into Australia to greatly influence the breed in that country.

In England, several other new kennels joined Darelyn in active breeding. Harkaway, Grinkle, Banworth, Burtoncurl, Siccawei, Renniston and Charcol all became important in the establishment of the breed as the Curly entered the second half of the 20th century.

Through the 1970s and 1980s, facing the growing popularity of the Labrador and the Flat Coat, the Curly's numbers continued to grow at a slow but steady rate. In historic moments for the breed, during the 1980s, Ch Darelyn Rifleman earned Best in Show wins over entries of 16,315 and 23,627 at England's largest dog

CURLIES IN AUSTRALIA

Breed history indicates presence of the Curly in Australia in the early 1800s. In 1897, Walter Bielby writes in *Dogs of Australia* about Martins Ravensdown Ben at a turn-of-the-century dog show in Victoria.

The Portuguese Water Dog derives from the same stock as most of the water-dog breeds.

today date back to the breeding of native Curlies to English imports. The very important dog, NZ and GFTCh Dual Ch Waitoki Tamatakapua, who is behind many modern Australian and New Zealand bloodlines, was the product of a New Zealand field trial champion and an English import bitch. Another significant pairing was that of English import Nelson Prince and his Australian-born daughter, Nelson Beauty. This breeding produced the important Australian Curly, Black Prince. Australian breeder Olaf Michelson of Victoria and his imported Tablik Curlies were the foundation of many of the country's homebred Curly Coated Retrievers.

shows. Not surprisingly, he became a dominant producer of important Curlies in England, Australia, the United States and continental Europe. Rifleman and his progeny can be found today in almost every Curly pedigree throughout those countries.

During the 1950s and 1960s, Australian breeders imported Darelyn Aristocrat from England, along with Sarona Simon, Banworth Simon, Banworth Athene and Pegasus, dogs who are behind over three-quarters of modern Curly bloodlines. The accomplished New Zealand import, Ch Waitoki Tuhora, QC, is also behind many of Australia's Curlies.

THE CURLY IN AUSTRALIA AND NEW ZEALAND

For over a century, Australians have prized the Curly Coated Retriever as a brave, intelligent and agile hunting dog. The sturdy Curly is often used to retrieve waterfowl as large as swans. Curlies have also been known to hunt Australian kangaroo, a feat that requires great courage as well as speed and natural hunting ability.

Most of the Curlies in Australia and New Zealand

As word of the Curly Coated Retriever spread across the Atlantic to North America, Australia began to export dogs to the United States and Canada, as well as to Germany, New Guinea and New Zealand, creating legions of new breed fanciers on other continents.

In New Zealand, the Curly Coated Retriever reigns, as the breed is the most popular hunting dog in that country. The Curly's intelligence, superb hunting ability and natural affinity for water earn the breed high marks with hunting enthusiasts and field trial aficionados.

Perhaps the most unusual aspect of the New Zealand Curly is its smaller size, with some breed specimens much smaller than the proper English Curly. This smaller version is a very popular duck dog, found mostly along the Murray River, where it is not surprisingly called the 'Murray River Curly.' The River Curlies are, for the most part, unregistered with The Kennel Club, and many River Curly fans feel it should be considered a separate breed.

THE CURLY IN THE UNITED STATES

Although America saw its first Curly Coated Retriever in 1907, the breed was not registered in the United States until 1924. Curly fanciers then were most enthusiastic about the breed's potential as a hunting dog; indeed, the breed prospered during the 1920s and 1930s, when they were popular as family pets as well as gundogs. Once again, World War II impacted the breed almost to the

point of total extinction, with only 16 specimens registered between 1941 and 1949. By 1950, when breeders of all breeds of dog were trying to re-establish their lines, the Labrador and Flat Coated Retriever had made huge inroads into the hunting populace, and many kennels began to produce faster and more stylish retrievers. Additionally, a rumour circulated in American dog circles that the Curly was hard-mouthed and that the breed's curly coat was difficult to maintain. Such false allegations led to a disastrous drop in Curly interest and support, reducing breed numbers to only two dogs registered in 1964. With a total lack of breeding stock, any remaining lines of Curly breeding stock were lost, and for a brief while the future of the breed looked bleak.

The resurrection came in 1964, when Mr Dale Dettweiler imported Eng Ch Siccawei Black Rod from England. This dog was affectionately called 'Limey' by those who judged him in the

THE COMMONER'S CURLY
The Curly in its native England was originally known as the commoner's or 'blue-collar' dog because the breed was more often owned by English gamekeepers or poachers than by the gentry or wealthy aristocrats.

Halling from the breed's homeland, Ch Gladrags Jackaranda is an excellent representative of what judges seek in the show ring for the Curly Coated Retriever. All champion Curly Coats must win in both the field and the show ring to earn the title.

show ring. Limey also worked in the field and had quite a loyal following of hunters who spent many successful hours hunting behind the dog. After this most successful import, Mr Dettwelier brought over more Curlies from England and Australia, and with those dogs he established his Curly kennel, bearing the prefix Windpatch. The Windpatch Curlies became the foundation for the breed in the United States, and Mr Dettweiler is considered by many to be the saviour of the modern American Curly.

As more dog fanciers became enamoured with the Curly Coated Retriever, more dogs were imported and several well-respected lines developed over the following 20 years. Breeders with the kennel prefixes of Summerwind, Severaven, Karakul, Charwin, Wits End, Ptarmigan, El Mack, Mayhem and Aarowag joined Mr Dettwelier on his mission to revitalise the breed.

By the mid-1970s, the Curly was solidly established in the United States, which led to the formation in 1979 of the Curly Coated Retriever Club of America. This club was later accepted by the American Kennel Club (AKC) as a licensed breed club. Although the organisation flourished, the breed is still somewhat rare in the US. By the mid-1990s, it was ranked at number 123 out of 137 AKC-registered breeds, and during the last decade of the 20th century, less than 200 Curlies were registered annually.

Although the breed is not numerous in most countries, locating a quality breeder should not be beyond the abilities of potential owners. Contacting the national kennel club or breed club is usually the recommended way of finding a breeder.

Underneath that unique curly coat is a temperament just as special.

PERSONALITY AND TEMPERAMENT

'Unique' may be the word to best describe the Curly Coated Retriever. His tightly curled, water-repellent coat is his most distinguishing characteristic, and

the one that most often generates questions and conversation. However, the dog beneath the coat is equally unique in temperament and ability. The Curly is a highly intelligent and independent retriever, considered by many to be the most intelligent, but also the most wilful, of all retriever breeds. Although (and because) they learn quickly, they also become bored very easily, which creates a training conundrum for the average owner or trainer who often tends to use repetitive techniques when training for simple obedience or everyday field work.

Highly intelligent and very independent, the Curly Coated Retriever is an active and inquisitive dog that demands much of the owner and trainer.

Despite the breed's seemingly hard-nosed qualities, the Curly's temperament is rather soft and yielding, and dominant or heavy-handed training approaches are rarely necessary. The Curly has a higher-than-average energy level and is more inquisitive than most other retrievers—two qualities that, combined, make for a very active dog in body and mind.

The Curly is a most loyal and gentle dog who makes an excellent family companion as well as a very capable gundog. Curlies are seldom aggressive with other dogs or animals. Adult Curlies are very gentle with youngsters, but because of their large size and great exuberance, they can sometimes be unintentionally rough in play and accidentally knock over small children. As with any other breed, Curlies should be supervised when playing or interacting with children.

Given their strong social tendencies, Curlies do not thrive in isolation or as garden or kennel dogs; rather, they do best when living as integral parts of family units. As family members, they are independent and discerning, perhaps sometimes appearing aloof and undemonstrative, especially with strangers. Because of his active nature, a Curly kept indoors should be well socialised and taught household manners from a

BARK!
The Curly is a discriminating barker who will bark at new or strange people or objects, but will not bark on endlessly. Intensely loyal to his family and loved ones, he is a good watchdog that can be trained or encouraged to be protective, but is not considered a natural protection breed.

very early age to help ensure his growth into a well-behaved canine citizen. Puppy socialisation class, progressing to basic obedience training, is necessary if you hope to live in harmony with your Curly.

The Curly has an excellent memory and a great capacity for learning, which makes training both fun and challenging. Another important fact that affects their training is that Curlies are known to be slower to mature than other retriever breeds. Thus, training sessions should be kept short, fun and interesting if you are to achieve long-term success in moulding adult behaviour. Their slow rate of maturity is a major factor in the working Curly, as few field trialers or professional trainers are interested in working with a dog who doesn't get serious about his work until he is three or four years old.

Curly Coated Retrievers are known to be clever and creative in their quest for mischief or

MALE OR FEMALE?
Regarding gender differences, some males may be more dominant and stronger willed, but this is more dependent on the individual personality of each male or female. Males are larger, usually outweighing the females by 4.5–9 kgs (10 to 20 pounds).

adventure. They require vigorous daily exercise to keep physically healthy and emotionally content. A garden with a six-foot fence is best for safe containment, as Curlies are quite adept at scaling lower fences. Also, while they are not known to be diggers, they will dig if bored. They are not road- or traffic-wise, so would be at great risk if permitted to roam freely about the neighbourhood.

PHYSICAL CHARACTERISTICS

Physically, the Curly is a large dog of sturdy structure who can weigh from 50 to 100 pounds, with males on the larger end of the spectrum. His very curly coat is his most unusual characteristic, composed of very small, hard, tight, waterproof curls that extend from the back of the head down to the elbows and hocks to the tip of the tail, with only the face devoid of any curls. Only his short facial hair grows straight and smooth. Curlies come in either black or liver, with black being the more predominant colour.

The Curly's coat is virtually briar-and-bramble-proof, and in most cases, the hard, tight curls

DID YOU KNOW?
Curlies are considered a slow-maturing breed. They are puppy-like until at least two years old, reaching physical and emotional maturity at about three-and-a-half years of age.

will not allow burrs or seeds to penetrate, a feature that is prized by hunters who work with the breed. In water, the coat is equally efficient, offering far better protection than the coats of his retriever relatives, the Golden, the Flat Coat and the Labrador. Hunters claim that, of all the retriever breeds, the Curly's coat offers the most ideal insulation and protection, keeping his skin warm and dry during a full day's shoot, especially important when hunting in bleak, icy winter conditions.

The distinctive coat is easy for the owner to maintain. It does not require daily care; nor should it be brushed or combed, as this would be detrimental to the tight curls. Only during the spring and

DID YOU KNOW?
Intact Curlies cast their coat just before every heat cycle. The coat will grow back within six to eight weeks after shedding.

MASTERS OF ESCAPE
Curlies are known to be masterful escape artists and, if left unsupervised, will work out how to escape from most fenced enclosures.

fall moulting periods does the coat need to be brushed. Shedding is not a problem with this breed, as throughout the rest of the year only slight routine shedding occurs.

Bathing is necessary three or four times a year, as the coats tends to get oily and gather dust and debris. For the allergic Curly owner, bathing the dog will get rid of potential irritants that have gathered in the coat. For working Curlies, even less frequent bathing is necessary. Swimming serves the same function as bathing in that the water removes dirt and dust from the coat.

However, any Curly used for water or field work should be checked often to ensure that no burrs, insects, etc, have taken up residence in the coat, ears or anywhere else on the body.

ENERGY AND ABILITY
Like his American descendant, the Chesapeake Bay Retriever, the Curly is exceptionally powerful for his size. Although not as fast or stylish as the Labrador or Golden Retriever, he nevertheless has tremendous endurance, working at a steady, sensible pace and never seeming to tire. Many hunters claim that the Curly's most remarkable quality is his perseverance; he just will not give up on a bird.

Curlies are exceptionally good swimmers, and they love to swim! Most will dive enthusiastically into any body of water at every opportunity. However, one should still exercise caution when introducing a puppy to water. Never throw or push a pup into the water; always allow him to approach and enter it when he feels ready to do so. He will soon gain confidence and be splashing about on his own.

GENE DROOL
Curlies are known to drool at times, a trait that may stem from their Newfoundland relatives.

Because it is a large-breed dog with a high energy level, a Curly Coated Retriever needs a securely fenced garden and an active family who will give its dog lots of daily exercise. With a Curly puppy, though, jumping and high-impact exercise should be avoided before one year of age to avoid stress on growing joints. Curly owners have the opportunity to participate in a wide range of activities with their dogs. The Curly Coated Retriever loves to take part in activities that allow him to expend some energy. Even better is if the activity allows him to make use of his instinctive abilities.

The Curly today still excels at the task for which he was intended—that of finding and retrieving game birds, both in water and on land. Hunters who work with their Curlies find the dogs to be tremendous assets, and many Curlies participate in organised field trial competition.

Aside from field work and trials, other popular activities for the Curly include working trials, obedience competition, agility trials and flyball. The most important key to success in training your Curly for anything is to start when the puppy is quite young. This will build a good foundation for your future together. Since that cute Curly puppy will mature into a large and rather wilful dog, the owner is wise to teach him basic

Because the Curly is single-coated, he sheds much less than other retriever breeds that have a double coat.

DOGS, DOGS, GOOD FOR YOUR HEART!

People usually purchase dogs for companionship, but studies show that dogs can help to improve their owners' health and level of activity, as well as lower a human's risk of coronary heart disease. Without even realising it, when a person puts time into exercising, grooming and feeding a dog, he also puts more time into his own personal health care. Dog owners establish more routine schedules for their dogs to follow, which can have positive effects on a human's health. Dogs also teach us patience, offer unconditional love and provide the joy of having a furry friend to pet!

obedience commands early on so he will grow into a responsive and well-behaved companion.

HEREDITARY HEALTH CONCERNS

Nearly every breed of dog is plagued by certain hereditary diseases, some of which are common to several types or groups of dogs. For example, like many modern dog breeds, the Curly Coated Retriever is experiencing a disturbing increase in the number of dogs who contract

various forms of malignant cancers. Other health problems are more breed-specific. Regardless, there a few health problems of which every Curly owner or prospective owner should be aware. While the majority of Curly Coated Retrievers will not be affected by health problems, owners who are informed of potential problems will be better able to notice the signs and provide their dogs with prompt veterinary care.

PATTERNED BALDNESS

The most widespread health problem in the Curly Coated Retriever is patterned baldness. This usually manifests itself in bilateral hair loss, meaning on both sides of the dog, with bald strips or patches appearing on the backs of the rear legs, on the neck, on the throat and behind the shoulders. Thin, brittle and uncurled hair is another common symptom. In mild cases, the patterning may appear only once and never again appear after the hair grows back. However, it is a symptom of a greater problem, as it is caused by an auto-immune deficiency. Affected dogs are more likely to have allergies, reproductive problems and growth hormone problems wherein the dog matures to only about 18 kgs (40 pounds).

An affected dog may have a good coat as a puppy, with bald spots developing when the dog reaches sexual maturity. Seemingly unaffected adults can produce patterned pups, so it is important for the breeder to know the genetics behind any dogs being used for breeding purposes.

Patterned baldness is easily and frequently misdiagnosed. Many veterinary surgeons are unfamiliar with this particular problem and can easily blame the bald spots on diet deficiency or wear from a too-wide collar. Unfortunately, special diets and

Like most other gundogs, the Curly Coat is a gregarious, friendly soul, able to get along with most other dogs. This veteran Curly is sharing a walk with a young German Wire-haired Pointer.

supplements do not help
patterned baldness.

Although the condition is not
life-threatening, and mildly
affected Curlies will live normal,
healthy lives, dogs affected to any
degree should not be bred.

Hip Dysplasia (HD)
Hip dysplasia means, quite
simply, poor or abnormal
formation of the hip joint. HD
most commonly occurs in large
breeds of dog and is known to be
inherited. A severe case can
render a hunting dog worthless in
the field, and even a mild case
can cause painful arthritic
changes in the average house dog.
Less severe cases may go
undetected until changes in the
dog's mobility indicate a problem.

HD is caused by several
recessive genes, which unfortunately means that dogs with
cleared (non-dysplastic) hips
could carry dysplastic genes that
may pass on to their progeny. HD
can be diagnosed only through x-
ray examination, and only by
screening several generations of
breeding stock can a breeder be
better assured of offspring with
healthy hips.

While hip dysplasia is largely
an inherited condition, research
shows that environmental factors
also play a significant part in its
development. Overfeeding and
feeding a diet high in calories
(primarily fat) during a puppy's

CORRECTIVE SURGERY
Surgery is often used to correct
genetic bone diseases in dogs. Usually
the problems present themselves
early in the dog's life and must be
treated before bone growth stops.

rapid-growth stages are suspected
to be contributing factors in the
development of HD. Heavy-bodied
and overweight puppies are more
at risk than pups with very lean
conformation.

In Great Britain, the British
Veterinary Association has joined
with The Kennel Club
(BVA/KC/HD) to help curb the
incidence of hip dysplasia in all
breeds of dog. Dogs over one year
and under six years of age should
be x-rayed by a veterinary
surgeon. The x-rays are submitted
to a special board of veterinary
surgeons who specialise in
reading orthopaedic films. X-rays
are assigned a score of 0 (which is
the minimum or best possible
score) up to 53 (the worst possible
score) for each hip, producing a
possible total score of 0 to 106. If
the dog shows no evidence of
abnormality, a certificate of
clearance is issued by The Kennel
Club.

To correctly identify the dog
under evaluation, The Kennel
Club requires the dog's date of
birth and Kennel Club registration number to be recorded on

DO YOU KNOW ABOUT HIP DYSPLASIA?

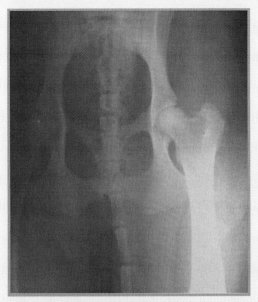

X-ray of a dog with 'Good' hips.

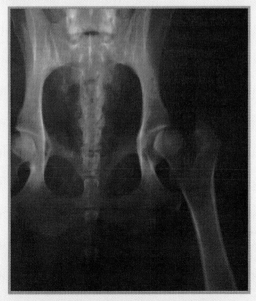

X-ray of a dog with 'Moderate' dysplastic hips.

Hip dysplasia is a fairly common condition found in pure-bred dogs. When a dog has hip dysplasia, its hind leg has an incorrectly formed hip joint. By constant use of the hip joint, it becomes more and more loose, wears abnormally and may become arthritic.

Hip dysplasia can only be confirmed with an x-ray, but certain symptoms may indicate a problem. Your dog may have a hip dysplasia problem if it walks in a peculiar manner, hops instead of smoothly runs, uses its hind legs in unison (to keep the pressure off the weak joint), has trouble getting up from a prone position or always sits with both legs together on one side of its body.

As the dog matures, it may adapt well to life with a bad hip, but in a few years the arthritis develops and many dogs with hip dysplasia become cripples.

Hip dysplasia is considered an inherited disease and only can be diagnosed definitively when the dog is two years old. Some experts claim that a special diet might help your puppy outgrow the bad hip, but the usual treatments are surgical. The removal of the pectineus muscle, the removal of the round part of the femur, reconstructing the pelvis and replacing the hip with an artificial one are all surgical interventions that are expensive, but they are usually very successful. Follow the advice of your veterinary surgeon.

the x-ray. The purpose of such screening is to eliminate affected dogs from breeding programmes with the long-term goal of reducing the incidence of hip dysplasia in affected breeds.

Curlies who show marked evidence of hip dysplasia should never be bred. Anyone looking for a healthy Curly puppy should make certain that the sire and dam of any litter under consideration have their certificates of clearance.

ELBOW DYSPLASIA (ED)

Like HD, elbow dysplasia is a developmental joint disease; ED affects the elbow. It involves several problems, including ununited anconeal process, fragmented cornoid process and osteochondritis dessicans. ED can be detected only through x-ray. While not a major problem in the Curly Coated Retriever, some are known to be affected, and affected dogs should not be bred.

EYE PROBLEMS

Progressive retinal atrophy (PRA), retinal dysplasia (RD) and several types of cataracts are hereditary eye conditions that can lead to vision problems later in a dog's life. While some cataracts do not interfere with a dog's vision, others can progress into complete or partial blindness. Fortunately, surgery is now available to correct some types of cataracts.

Cataracts can be diagnosed by a veterinary ophthalmic examination as early as six months of age. Eyes should be examined annually until at least eight years of age, as some cataracts can occur later in the dog's life. All Curlies should be cleared before breeding, and affected animals should not be bred.

PRA and RD are inherited defects of the retina (or light receptor area of the eye). These conditions can be diagnosed only through ophthalmic examination by a veterinary surgeon. Unlike the progressive deterioration that occurs with PRA, RD does not result in total blindness; instead, it will affect a working dog's ability to function at a chosen task. Dogs afflicted with either condition should be removed from breeding programmes.

An owner wishing to certify his dog as free from hereditary cataracts, PRA and RD must be referred to a referee by the examining veterinary surgeon. The referee will examine the dog and review the veterinary transfer certificate as well as the dog's Kennel Club registration certificate. The referee signs his report, gives one copy to the owner, sends a copy to the British Veterinary Association and keeps one copy for himself. If the report is favourable, The Kennel Club will then issue a permanent or interim certificate of clearance.

Discuss the occurrence of eye problems with your chosen breeder. All breeding stock should be screened for potential problems, and no visually impaired dogs should ever be bred.

Profile head study of a quality Curly. The hair on the face should be smooth and straight, in contrast to the the body coat's tight curls.

To fully appreciate the elements of any breed standard, one must first understand why a standard is necessary in the first place. In order to preserve a breed's unique characteristics, the original breed specialists who formed the breed's parent club(s) adopted a standard, for without a detailed description to use as a guideline for future breedings, many of the breed's valued qualities could easily become weakened or lost completely. The Curly was developed over many decades by fanciers and hunters who prized this breed for those special qualities that best served their needs and desires, whether working in the water, retrieving in the field or spending time in the home. Therefore, the intent of the Curly standard is to preserve and promote the integrity of every aspect of the breed.

The breed standard describes the perfect dog and is used by breeders and by judges as a 'yardstick' to measure dogs competing in shows.

THE KENNEL CLUB STANDARD FOR THE RETRIEVER (CURLY COATED)

General Appearance: Strong, active, smart, upstanding, with distinctive coat.

Characteristics: Intelligent with endurance.

Temperament: Friendly and confident.

Head and Skull: Long, well proportioned flat skull, jaws strong and long without snipiness

Correctly proportioned flat skull with rather small, low-set ears.

Incorrect rounded skull with too-large ears.

Correct rear, with proper tailset and hocks low to ground.

Poor rear, with bad tailset and weak hocks.

Correct hindquarters.

Poor hindquarters, 'cowhocks.'

Correct tail, carried straight, tapering to a point.

Incorrect tail, carried in a curl.

or coarseness. Wide nostrils, black or liver pigment.

Eyes: Black or dark brown, large but not prominent.

Ears: Rather small, set on low, lying close to head, covered with short curls.

Mouth: Jaws strong and level with perfect, regular and complete scissor bite, i.e. upper teeth closely overlapping lower teeth and set square to the jaws.

Neck: Moderately long, free from throatiness.

Forequarters: Shoulders very deep, muscular. Well laid back.

Body: Well sprung ribs, good depth of brisket, not long in loin or tucked up.

Hindquarters: Strong, muscular, hock low to ground and well bent.

Feet: Round, compact, toes well arched.

Tail: Moderately short, carried straight, covered with curls, tapering towards point, never gay or curled.

Gait/Movement: Covering plenty of ground with drive.

Coat: Mass of crisp, small curls all

over, the main characteristic of the breed and of supreme importance.

Colour: Black or liver.

Size: Desirable height at withers: dogs: 69 cms (27 ins); bitches: 64 cms (25 ins).

Faults: Any departure from the foregoing points should be considered a fault and the seriousness with which the fault should be regarded should be in exact proportion to its degree.

Note: Male animals should have two apparently normal testicles fully descended into the scrotum.

BREEDING CONSIDERATIONS

The decision to breed your dog is one that must be considered carefully and researched thoroughly before moving into action. Some people believe that breeding will make their bitches happier or that it is an easy way to make money. Unfortunately, indiscriminate breeding only worsens the rampant problem of pet overpopulation, as well as putting a considerable dent in your pocketbook. As for the bitch, the entire process from mating through whelping is not an easy one and puts your pet under considerable stress. Last, but not least, consider whether or not you have the means to care for an entire litter of pups. Without a reputation in the field, your attempts to sell the pups may be unsuccessful, especially with an uncommon breed.

The word 'puppy' defines the Curly for the first few years of life…are you up to the challenge? If so, you will reap the rewards of everything this one-of-a-kind breed has to offer.

CURLY COATED RETRIEVER

FINDING A BREEDER

The puppy selection process for Curly Coated Retrievers is quite the same as with most breeds of dog. A reputable breeder is the most reliable source for a

Meeting the puppy face to face is a basic requirement when selecting the right Curly for you.

quality pup who is healthy and will possess the qualities typical of the breed. Because the breed is numerically small in most countries, finding a good breeder may be a challenge, but a long and happy future with your puppy is worth the extra effort involved in seeking out a responsible puppy source. Veterinary surgeons, breed and kennel clubs, dog shows and outdoor field events are all good sources of information about the breed and breeders.

Once you have located a trustworthy breeder, both you and the breeder should have questions about each other. Your concern is the health and stability of the pups, and the breeder should be interested in you as a dog owner and what kind of home you will provide for the little one. If the breeder fails to make any enquiries about you and is willing to sell you a puppy without asking any questions, you would be wise to look elsewhere for a pup.

Breeders typically want to know where the dog will live, who will care for it, where and how the dog will exercise, what other pets you own or have owned, how many children are in the house, why you want a Curly

able about the breed and is he involved in some element of competition or activity with his dogs? Does he belong to a breed or kennel club?

• Does the breeder have only one or two breeds of dog? Does he have only one, perhaps two litters at a time? If there are several breeds of dog, the breeder cannot devote sufficient time to becoming

The breeder should have at least one of the parents available for you to meet. The temperament and appearance of the sire and the dam will greatly reflect how your puppy will look and act as an adult.

Coated Retriever and how much time you have to devote to the dog. The breeder should also discuss health and genetic problems within the breed, especially any in his own lines. No breed is problem-free; if the breeder makes such a claim, it is best to move on in your puppy search.

The breeder should be able to provide answers to the following questions:

• Do both parents have hip clearances from the hip registry of their respective country? A statement from a veterinary surgeon is not a valid clearance.

• Have both parents been examined for hereditary eye disease by a qualified veterinary surgeon?

• How often is the dam bred? If bred every heat cycle, this is too often and may indicate that profit is the breeder's primary motive.

• Is the breeder knowledge-

PREPARING FOR PUP

Unfortunately, when a puppy is bought by someone who does not take into consideration the time and attention that dog ownership requires, it is the puppy who suffers when he is either abandoned or placed in a shelter by a frustrated owner. So all of the 'homework' you do in preparation for your pup's arrival will benefit you both. The more informed you are, the more you will know what to expect and the better equipped you will be to handle the ups and downs of raising a puppy. Hopefully, everyone in the household is willing to do his part in raising and caring for the pup. The anticipation of owning a dog often brings a lot of promises from excited family members: 'I will walk him every day,' 'I will feed him,' 'I will house-train him,' etc., but these things take time and effort, and promises can easily be forgotten once the novelty of the new pet has worn off.

really knowledgeable about each breed. If there is more than one litter, it is equally difficult to give the pups the time and attention that they need.

• Is the breeder willing to provide you with references of other people who have purchased puppies from him?

• Does the breeder have a written contract, and does the contract include a breeding restriction with a mandatory spay/neuter provision for pet dogs?

• Does the breeder guarantee the health of this puppy, and for how long, and will he take it back at any time for any reason if you cannot keep it? (This is the ultimate hallmark of responsible breeding.) Does the contract offer another puppy or money back in case of health or other problems with the puppy? Many unscrupulous breeders will honour guarantees only after the puppy is destroyed, asserting that they will never have to replace sick puppies.

• Why did the breeder plan this particular breeding between this sire and dam? 'He (or she) is a very sweet dog' or similar evasive answer is not sufficient reason to breed an animal.

• Can you meet the parents of the litter? The dam should most certainly be available and, if the sire is not, you should be able to view photos and paperwork on the sire.

PUPPY APPEARANCE
Your puppy should have a well-fed appearance but not a distended abdomen, which may indicate worms or incorrect feeding, or both. The body should be firm, with a solid feel. The skin of the abdomen should be pale pink and clean, without signs of scratching or rash. Check the hind legs to make certain that dewclaws were removed, if any were present at birth.

• Will the breeder provide you with a copy of a three- to five-generation pedigree? Does the pedigree contain any titles before or after the dogs' names (e.g. Ch, CC, OTCh, CD, JH, WC) in the first two generations? The term 'championship lines' is meaningless if those titles are three or

DID YOU KNOW?
You should not even think about buying a puppy that looks sick, undernourished, overly frightened or nervous. Sometimes a timid puppy will warm up to you after a 30-minute 'let's-get-acquainted' session.

BOY OR GIRL?
An important consideration to be discussed is the sex of your puppy. For a family companion, a bitch may be the better choice, considering the female's inbred concern for all young creatures and her accompanying tolerance and patience. It is always advisable to spay a pet bitch, which may guarantee her a longer life.

more generations back in any pedigree.

• Have the pups been raised in the home, not isolated in a kennel building or barn, and have they been socialised with other people, adults and children alike?

• Do the pups seem healthy, with no discharge from their eyes or noses, no loose stools, no foul-smelling ears? Are their coats healthy and clean? Do they appear energetic and playful when awake? Are they happy and confident around visitors, not cringing, timid or fearful?

• Have the pups been wormed, had their first shots, been checked by a veterinary surgeon? Does the breeder provide copies of health records and health clearances as well as literature to help you with feeding, house-training and obedience training?

• Do you feel comfortable with the breeder? Do you feel pressured or intimidated? Can you ask him questions without feeling like you are stupid or imposing?

Will he be available to answer questions at any time for the life of this dog?

SELECTING A PUPPY

Once you have contacted and met a breeder or two and made your choice about which breeder is best suited to your needs, it's time to visit the litter. Keep in mind that many top breeders have waiting lists, though this is not likely with an uncommon breed like the Curly Coated Retriever.

Once you've located a litter, you will have a good selection from which to choose; Curly litters average about six pups, some being as large as eight or nine. Since you are likely to be choosing a Curly as a pet dog and not a field or show dog, you simply should select a pup that is friendly, attractive and healthy. If you are selecting a Curly for hunting or field trialing, you are well advised to buy the pup from a breeder whose dogs are accomplished in gundog activities. Always check the bite of your selected puppy to be sure that it is neither overshot nor undershot. This may not be too noticeable on a young puppy, but will become more evident as the puppy gets older.

Breeders commonly allow visitors to see their litters by around the fifth or sixth week, and puppies leave for their new homes between the eighth and tenth week. Breeders who permit their puppies to leave early are more interested in your pounds

PUPPY SELECTION

Your selection of a good puppy can be determined by your needs. A show potential, a field dog or a good pet? It is your choice. Every puppy, however, should be of good temperament. Although show-quality puppies are bred and raised with emphasis on physical conformation, responsible breeders strive for equally good temperament and working qualities. Do not buy from a breeder who concentrates solely on physical beauty at the expense of all else.

The acquisition of any dog, particularly an intelligent and active breed like the Curly, requires the cooperation and consent of the whole family. Everyone must participate in the selection, care and training of the puppy.

than in their puppies' well-being. Puppies need to learn the rules of the pack from their dams, and most dams continue teaching the pups manners and dos and don'ts until around the eighth week. Breeders spend significant amounts of time with the Curly toddlers so that the pups are able

DOCUMENTATION

Two important documents you will get from the breeder are the pup's pedigree and registration certificate. The breeder should register the litter and each pup with The Kennel Club, and it is necessary for you to have the paperwork if you plan on showing or breeding in the future.

Make sure you know the breeder's intentions on which type of registration he will obtain for the pup. There are limited registrations which may prohibit the dog from being shown, bred or competing in non-conformation trials such as Working or Agility if the breeder feels that the pup is not of sufficient quality to do so. There is also a type of registration that will permit the dog in non-conformation competition only.

On the reverse side of the registration certificate, the new owner can find the transfer section, which must be signed by the breeder.

to interact with the 'other species,' i.e. humans. Given the long history that dogs and humans have, bonding between the two species is natural but must be nurtured. A well-bred, well-socialised Curly pup wants nothing more than to be near you and please you.

COMMITMENT OF OWNERSHIP
After considering all of these factors, you have most likely already made some very important decisions about selecting your puppy. You have

chosen a Curly Coated Retriever, which means that you have decided which characteristics you want in a dog and what type of dog will best fit into your family and lifestyle. If you have selected a breeder, you have gone a step further—you have done your research and found a responsible, conscientious person who breeds quality Curly Coated Retrievers and who should become a reliable source of help as you and your puppy adjust to life together. If you have observed a litter in action, you have obtained a firsthand look at the dynamics of a puppy 'pack' and, thus, you have learned about each pup's individual personality—perhaps you have even found one that particularly appeals to you.

However, even if you have not yet found the Curly puppy of your dreams, observing pups will help you learn to recognise certain behaviour and to determine what a pup's behaviour indicates about his temperament. You will be able to pick out which pups are the leaders, which ones are less outgoing, which ones are confident, which ones are shy, playful, friendly, aggressive, etc. Equally as important, you will learn to recognise what a healthy pup should look and act like. All of these things will help you in your search, and when you find the Curly Coated Retriever that was meant for you, you will know it!

Researching your breed, selecting a responsible breeder and observing as many pups as

DID YOU KNOW?
Breeders rarely release puppies until they are eight to ten weeks of age. This is an acceptable age for most breeds of dog, excepting toy breeds, which are not released until around 12 weeks, given their petite sizes. If a breeder has a puppy that is 12 weeks of age or older, it is likely well socialised and house-trained. Be sure that it is otherwise healthy before deciding to take it home.

PUPPY PERSONALITY
When a litter becomes available to you, choosing a pup out of all those adorable faces will not be an easy task! Sound temperament is of utmost importance, but each pup has its own personality and some may be better suited to you than others. A feisty, independent pup will do well in a home with older children and adults, while quiet, shy puppies will thrive in a home with minimal noise and distractions. Your breeder knows the pups best and should be able to guide you in the right direction.

possible are all important steps on the way to dog ownership. It may seem like a lot of effort...and you have not even taken the pup home yet! Remember, though, you cannot be too careful when it comes to deciding on the type of dog you want and finding out about your prospective pup's background. Buying a puppy is not—or should not be—just another whimsical purchase. This is one instance in which you actually do get to choose your own family. You may be thinking that buying a puppy should be fun—it should not be so serious and so much work. Keep in mind that your puppy is not a cuddly stuffed toy or decorative lawn ornament; rather, he is a living creature that will become a real member of your family for the next 10 to 12 years. You will come to realise that, while buying a puppy is a pleasurable and exciting endeavour, it is not something to be taken lightly. Relax...the fun will start when the pup comes home!

Always keep in mind that a puppy is nothing more than a baby in a furry disguise...a baby who is virtually helpless in a human world and who trusts his owner for fulfilment of his basic needs for survival. In addition to food, water and shelter, your pup needs care, protection, guidance and love. If you are not prepared to commit to this, then you are not prepared to own a dog.

Wait a minute, you say. How hard could this be? All of my neighbours own dogs and they seem to be doing just fine. Why should I have to worry about all of this? Well, you should not worry about it; in fact, you will probably find that once your Curly pup gets used to his new home, he will fall into his place in the family quite naturally. However, it never hurts to emphasise the commitment of dog ownership. With some time and patience, it is really not too difficult to raise a curious and exuberant Curly pup to be a well-adjusted and well-mannered adult dog—a dog that could be your most loyal friend.

INHERIT THE MIND
In order to know whether or not a puppy will fit into your lifestyle, you need to assess his personality. A good way to do this is to interact with his parents. Your pup inherits not only his appearance but also his personality and temperament from the sire and dam. If the parents are fearful or overly aggressive, these same traits may likely show up in your puppy.

PREPARING PUPPY'S PLACE IN YOUR HOME

Researching your breed and finding a breeder are only two aspects of the 'homework' you will have to do before taking your Curly Coated Retriever puppy home. You will also have to prepare your home and family for the new addition. Much as you would prepare a nursery for a newborn baby, you will need to designate a place in your home

Your local pet shop will have a suitable display of crates from which you can choose the crate most suitable for your needs.

that will be the puppy's own. How you prepare your home will depend on how much freedom the dog will be allowed. Whatever you decide, you must ensure that he has a place that he can 'call his own.'

When you bring your new puppy into your home, you are bringing him into what will become his home as well. Obviously, you did not buy a puppy with the intentions of catering to his every whim and allowing him to 'rule the roost,' but in order for a puppy to grow

into a stable, well-adjusted dog, he has to feel comfortable in his surroundings. Remember, he is leaving the warmth and security of his mother and littermates, as well as the familiarity of the only place he has ever known, so it is important to make his transition as easy as possible. By preparing a place in your home for the puppy, you are making him feel as welcome as possible in a strange new place. It should not take him long to get used to it, but the sudden shock of being transplanted is somewhat traumatic for a young pup. Imagine how a small child would feel in the same situation—that is how your puppy must be feeling. It is up to you to reassure him and to let him know, 'Little chap, you are going to like it here!'

WHAT YOU SHOULD BUY

CRATE
To someone unfamiliar with the use of crates in dog training, it may seem like punishment to shut a dog in a crate, but this is not the case at all. Although all breeders do not advocate crate training, more and more breeders and trainers are recommending crates as preferred tools for show and field puppies as well as pet puppies.

Crates are not cruel—crates have many humane and highly effective uses in dog care and training. For example, crate training is a popular and successful house-training method. In addition, a crate can keep your dog safe during travel and, perhaps most importantly, a crate provides your dog with a place of his own in your home. It serves as a 'doggie bedroom' of sorts—your Curly Coated Retriever can curl up in his crate when he wants to sleep or when he just needs a break. Many dogs sleep in their crates overnight. With soft bedding and his favourite toy, a crate becomes a cosy pseudo-den for your dog. Like his ancestors, he too will seek out the comfort and retreat of a den—you just happen to be providing him with something a little more luxurious than what his early ancestors enjoyed.

As far as purchasing a crate, the type that you buy is up to you. It will most likely be one of the two most popular types: wire or fibreglass. There are advantages and disadvantages to each type. For example, a wire crate is more open, allowing the air to flow through and affording the dog a

CRATE TRAINING TIPS

During crate training, you should partition off the section of the crate in which the pup stays. If he is given too big an area, this will hinder your training efforts. Crate training is based on the fact that a dog does not like to soil his sleeping quarters, so it is ineffective to keep a pup in a crate that is so big that he can eliminate in one end and get far enough away from it to sleep. Also, you want to make the crate den-like for the pup. Blankets and a favourite toy will make the crate cosy for the small pup; as he grows, you may want to evict some of his 'roommates' to make more room.

It will take some coaxing at first, but be patient. Given some time to get used to it, your pup will adapt to his new home-within-a-home quite nicely.

ARE YOU A FIT OWNER?

If the breeder from whom you are buying a puppy asks you a lot of personal questions, do not be insulted. Such a breeder wants to be sure that you will be a fit provider for his puppy.

view of what is going on around him, while a fibreglass crate is sturdier. Both can double as travel crates, providing protection for the dog. The size of the crate is another thing to consider. Puppies do not stay puppies forever—in

PLAY'S THE THING

Teaching the Curly to play with his toys in running and fetching games is an ideal way to help the dog develop muscle, learn motor skills and bond with you, his owner and master.

He also needs to learn how to inhibit his bite reflex and never to use his teeth on people, forbidden objects and other animals in play. Whenever you play with your dog, you make the rules. This becomes an important message to your Curly in teaching him that you are the pack leader and control everything he does in life. Once your dog accepts you as his leader, your relationship with him will be cemented for life.

fact, sometimes it seems as if they grow right before your eyes. A small crate may be fine for a very young Curly pup, but it will not do him much good for long! Unless you have the money and the inclination to buy a new crate every time your pup has a growth spurt, it is better to get one that will accommodate your dog both as a pup and at full size. A rather large crate will be necessary for a fully-grown Curly Coated Retriever, who stands approximately 64–69 cms (25–27 ins) high.

BEDDING
Veterinary bedding in the dog's crate will help the dog feel more at home, and you may also like to pop in a small blanket. First, this will take the place of the leaves, twigs, etc., that the pup would use in the wild to make a den; the pup can make his own 'burrow' in the crate. Although your pup is far removed from his den-making ancestors, the denning instinct is still a part of his genetic makeup. Second, until you take your pup home, he has been sleeping amidst the warmth of his mother and littermates, and while a blanket is not the same as a warm, breathing body, it still provides heat and something with which to snuggle. You will want to wash your pup's bedding frequently in case he has a toileting 'accident' in his crate, and replace or remove any blanket that becomes ragged and starts to fall apart.

TOYS
Toys are a must for dogs of all ages, especially for curious playful pups. Puppies are the

'children' of the dog world, and what child does not love toys? Chew toys provide enjoyment for both dog and owner—your dog will enjoy playing with his favourite toys, while you will enjoy the fact that they distract him from chewing on your expensive shoes and leather sofa. Puppies love to chew; in fact, chewing is a physical need for pups as they are teething, and everything looks appetising! The full range of your possessions—from old tea towel to Oriental carpet—are fair game in the eyes of a teething pup. Puppies are not all that discerning when it comes to finding something literally to 'sink their teeth into'—everything tastes great!

Like all retriever breeds, Curlies like to chew. Only strong, sturdy toys should be offered to Curly Coated Retrievers, puppies or adults. Hard sterile bones, nylon bones, large raw knuckle bones and other hard chew devices are safe and satisfying choices. Breeders advise owners to resist stuffed toys, because they can become de-stuffed in no time. The overly excited pup may ingest the stuffing, which is not digestible. Similarly, squeaky toys are quite popular, but must be avoided for the Curly Coated Retriever. Perhaps a squeaky toy can be used as an aid in training, but not for free play. If a pup 'disembowels' one of these, the

TOYS, TOYS, TOYS!

With a big variety of dog toys available, and so many that look like they would be a lot of fun for a dog, be careful in your selection. It is amazing what a set of puppy teeth can do to an innocent-looking toy, so, obviously, safety is a major

consideration. Be sure to choose the most durable products that you can find. Hard nylon bones and toys are a safe bet, and many of them are offered in different scents and flavours that will be sure to capture your dog's attention. It is always fun to play a game of catch with your dog, and there are balls and flying discs that are specially made to withstand dog teeth.

Your local pet shop should have many leads from which you can select the lead best suited for your Curly.

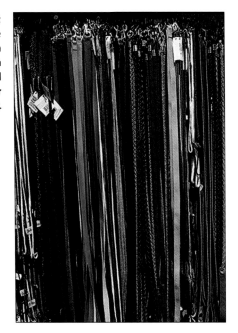

small plastic squeaker inside can be dangerous if swallowed. Monitor the condition of all your pup's toys carefully and get rid of any that have been chewed to the point of becoming potentially dangerous.

Be careful of natural bones, which have a tendency to splinter into sharp, dangerous pieces. Also be careful of rawhide, which can turn into pieces that are easy to swallow and become a mushy mess on your carpet.

LEAD

A nylon lead is probably the best option, as it is the most resistant to puppy teeth should your pup take a liking to chewing on his lead. Of course, this is a habit that should be nipped in the bud, but, if your pup likes to chew on his lead, he has a very slim chance of being able to chew through the strong nylon. Nylon leads are also lightweight, which is good for a young Curly who is just getting used to the idea of walking on a lead. For everyday walking and safety purposes, the nylon lead is a good choice. As your pup grows up and gets used to walking on the lead, you may want to purchase a flexible lead. These leads allow you to extend the length to give the dog a broader area to explore or to shorten the length to keep the dog near you. Of course, there are leads designed for training purposes

FINANCIAL RESPONSIBILITY

Grooming tools, collars, leashes, dog beds and, of course, toys will be an expense to you when you first obtain your pup, and the cost will continue throughout your dog's lifetime. If your puppy damages or destroys your possessions (as most puppies surely will!) or something belonging to a neighbour, you can calculate additional expense. There is also flea and pest control, which every dog owner faces more than once. You must be able to handle the financial responsibility of owning a dog.

CHOOSE AN APPROPRIATE COLLAR

The **BUCKLE COLLAR** is the standard collar used for everyday purposes. Be sure that you adjust the buckle on growing puppies. Check it every day. It can become too tight overnight! These collars can be made of leather or nylon. Attach your dog's identification tags to this collar.

The **CHOKE COLLAR** is constructed of highly polished steel so that it slides easily through the stainless steel loop. The idea is that the dog controls the pressure around its neck and he will stop pulling if the collar becomes uncomfortable. Never leave a choke collar on your dog when not training. This collar is not recommended for coated breeds, nor is it a recommended training tool for the Curly.

The **HALTER** is for a trained dog that has to be restrained to prevent running away, chasing a cat and the like. Considered the most humane of all collars, it is frequently used on smaller dogs for which collars are not comfortable.

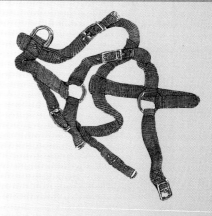

Purchase durable food and water bowls for your dog. There should be a wide selection at your pet-supply outlet.

PHOTO COURTESY OF MIKKI PET PRODUCTS.

and specially made leather harnesses, but these are not necessary for routine walks.

COLLAR

Your pup should get used to wearing a collar all the time since you will want to attach his ID tags to it; plus, you have to attach the lead to something! A lightweight nylon collar is a good choice. Make certain that the collar fits snugly enough so that the pup cannot wriggle out of it, but is loose enough so that it will not be uncomfortably tight around the pup's neck. You should be able to fit a finger between the pup's neck and the collar. It may take some time for your pup to get used to wearing the collar, but soon he will not even notice that it is there. Choke collars are made for training, but should only be used by experienced handlers. Such a training method should not be necessary with a Curly Coated Retriever.

FOOD AND WATER BOWLS

Your pup will need two bowls, one for food and one for water. You may want two sets of bowls, one for indoors and one for outdoors, depending on where the dog will be fed and where he will be spending time. Stainless steel or sturdy plastic bowls are popular choices. Plastic bowls are more chewable, but dogs tend not to chew on the steel variety, which can be sterilised. It is important to buy sturdy bowls since anything is in danger of being chewed by puppy teeth and you do not want your dog to be constantly chewing apart his bowl (for his safety and for your purse!).

CLEANING SUPPLIES
Until a pup is house-trained, you will be doing a lot of cleaning. 'Accidents' will occur, which is acceptable in the beginning stages of toilet training because the puppy does not know any better. All you can do is be prepared to clean up any accidents as soon as they happen. Old rags, towels, newspapers and a safe disinfectant are good to have on hand.

BEYOND THE BASICS
The items previously discussed are the bare necessities. You will find out what else you need as you go along—grooming supplies, flea/tick protection, baby gates to partition a room, etc. These things will vary depending on your situation, but it is important that you have everything you need to feed and make your Curly Coated Retriever comfortable in his first few days at home.

PUPPY-PROOFING YOUR HOME
Aside from making sure that your Curly will be comfortable in your home, you also have to make sure that your home is safe for your

It is your responsibility to clean up after your dog has relieved himself. Pet shops sell various aids to assist in the clean-up task.

Curly. This means taking precautions that your pup will not get into anything he should not get into and that there is nothing within his reach that may harm him should he sniff it, chew it, inspect it, etc. This probably seems obvious since, while you are primarily concerned with your pup's safety, at the same time you do not want your belongings to be ruined. Breakables should be placed out of reach if your dog is to have full run of the house. If he is to be limited to certain places within the house, keep any potentially dangerous items in the 'off-limits' areas.

An electrical cord can pose a danger should the puppy decide to taste it—and who is going to convince a pup that it would not

NATURAL TOXINS

Examine your grass and garden landscaping before bringing your Curly home. Many varieties of plants have leaves, stems or flowers that are toxic if ingested, and you can depend on a curious Curly to investigate them. Ask your vet for information on poisonous plants or research them at your library.

should be granted that freedom. Do not let a fence give you a false sense of security, as Curlies are known for their expertise at the art of escape. You would be surprised at how crafty (and persistent) a Curly can be in working out how to dig and squeeze his way through holes or to jump or climb over a fence. The remedy is to make the fence well embedded into the ground and high enough so that it really is impossible for your dog to get over it (about 6 feet should suffice). Be sure to repair or secure any gaps in the fence. Check the fence periodically to ensure that it is in good shape and make repairs as needed; a very determined pup may return to the same spot to 'work on it' until he is able to get through.

make a great chew toy? Cords should be fastened tightly against the wall. If your dog is going to spend time in a crate, make sure that there is nothing near his crate that he can reach if he sticks his curious little nose or paws through the openings. Just as you would with a child, keep all household cleaners and chemicals where the pup cannot reach them.

It is also important to make sure that the outside of your home is safe. Of course, your puppy should never be unsupervised, but a pup let loose in the garden will want to run and explore, and he

FIRST TRIP TO THE VET

You have selected your puppy, and your home and family are ready. Now all you have to do is collect your Curly Coated Retriever from the breeder and the fun begins, right? Well…not so fast. Something else you need to plan is your pup's first trip to the veterinary surgeon. Perhaps the breeder can recommend someone in the area who specialises in the retriever breeds, or maybe you know some other Curly owners who can suggest a good vet. Either way, you should have an appointment arranged for your pup before you pick him up.

The pup's first visit will consist of an overall examination to make sure that the pup does not have any problems that are not apparent to you. The veterinary surgeon will also set up a schedule for the pup's vaccinations; the breeder will inform you of which ones the pup has already received and the vet can continue from there.

INTRODUCTION TO THE FAMILY

Everyone in the house will be excited about the puppy's coming home and will want to pet him and play with him, but it is best to keep the introductions low-key so as not to overwhelm the puppy. He is apprehensive already. It is the first time he has been separated from his mother and the breeder, and the ride to your home is likely to be the first time he has been in a car. The last thing you want to do is smother him, as this will only frighten him further. This is not to say that human contact is not extremely necessary at this stage, because this is the time when a connection between the pup and his human family is formed. Gentle petting and soothing words should help console him, as well as just putting him down and letting him explore on his own (under your watchful eye, of course).

The pup may approach the

family members or may busy himself with exploring for a while. Gradually, each person should spend some time with the pup, one at a time, crouching down to get as close to the pup's level as possible, letting him sniff their hands and petting him gently. He definitely needs human attention and he needs to be touched—this is how to form an immediate bond. Just remember that the pup is experiencing many things for the first time, at the same time. There are new people, new noises, new smells and new things to investigate, so be gentle, be affectionate and be as comforting as you can be.

PUPPY-PROOFING

Thoroughly puppy-proof your house before bringing your puppy home. Never use cockroach or rodent poisons in any area accessible to the puppy. Avoid the use of toilet cleaners. Most dogs are born with 'toilet sonar' and will take a drink if the lid is left open. Also keep the rubbish secured and out of reach.

PUP'S FIRST NIGHT HOME

You have travelled home with your new charge safely in his crate. He's been to the vet for a thorough check-up; he's been weighed, his papers have been examined and perhaps he's even been vaccinated and wormed as well. He's met (and licked!) the whole family, including the excited children and the less-than-happy cat. He's explored his area, his new bed, the garden and anywhere else he's been permitted. He's eaten his first meal at home and relieved

CHEMICAL TOXINS

Scour your garage for potential puppy dangers. Remove weed killers, pesticides and antifreeze materials. Antifreeze is highly toxic and even a few drops can kill a dog, puppy or adult. The sweet taste attracts the animal, who will quickly consume it from the floor or curbside.

himself in the proper place. He's heard lots of new sounds, smelled new friends and seen more of the outside world than ever before... and that was just the first day! He's worn out and is ready for bed...or so you think!

It's puppy's first night home and you are ready to say 'Good night.' Keep in mind that this is his first night ever to be sleeping alone. His dam and littermates are no longer at paw's length and he's a bit scared, cold and lonely. Be reassuring to your new family member, but this is not the time to spoil him and give in to his inevitable whining.

Puppies whine. They whine to let others know where they are and hopefully to get company out of it. Place your pup in his new bed or crate in his designated area and close the door. Mercifully, he may fall asleep without a peep. When the inevitable occurs, however, ignore the whining—he is fine. Be strong and keep his interest in mind. Do not allow

TOXIC PLANTS

Many plants can be toxic to dogs. If you see your dog carrying a piece of vegetation in his mouth, approach him in a quiet, disinterested manner, avoid eye contact, pet him and gradually remove the plant from his mouth. Alternatively, offer him a treat and maybe he'll drop the plant on his own accord. Be sure no toxic plants are growing in your own garden.

yourself to feel guilty and visit the pup. He will fall asleep eventually.

Many breeders recommend placing a piece of bedding from the pup's former home in his new bed so that he recognises and is comforted by the scent of his littermates. Others still advise placing a hot water bottle in the bed for warmth. The latter may be a good idea provided the pup doesn't attempt to suckle—he'll get good and wet, and may not fall asleep so fast.

Puppy's first night can be somewhat stressful for both the pup and his new family. Remember that you are setting the tone of night-time at your house. Unless you want to play with your pup every night at 10 p.m., midnight and 2 a.m., don't initiate the habit. Your family will thank you, and so will your pup!

PREVENTING PUPPY PROBLEMS

SOCIALISATION

Now that you have done all of the preparatory work and have helped your pup get accustomed to his new home and family, it is about time for you to have some fun! Socialising your Curly pup gives you the opportunity to show off your new friend, and your pup gets to reap the benefits of being an adorable furry creature that people will want to pet and, in general, think is absolutely precious!

Besides getting to know his new family, your puppy should be exposed to other people, animals and situations. This will help him become well adjusted as he grows up and less prone to being timid

HOW VACCINES WORK

If you've just bought a puppy, you surely know the importance of having your pup vaccinated, but do you understand how vaccines work? Vaccines contain the same bacteria or viruses that cause the disease you want to prevent, but they have been chemically modified so that they don't cause any harm. Instead, the vaccine causes your dog to produce antibodies that fight the harmful bacteria. Thus, if your pup is exposed to the disease in the future, the antibodies will destroy the viruses or bacteria.

The breeder's rapport with her puppies will tell you a lot about how the litter has been cared for. Dedication to and love of the breed are evident in how the puppies respond to the breeder's attention.

or fearful of the new things he will encounter. Of course, he must not come into close contact with dogs you don't know well until his course of injections is fully complete.

Your pup's socialisation began with the breeder, but now it is your responsibility to continue it. The socialisation he receives until the age of 12 weeks is the most critical, as this is the time when he forms his impressions of the outside world. Be especially careful during the eight-to-ten-

week period, also known as the fear period. The interaction he receives during this time should be gentle and reassuring. Lack of socialisation, and/or negative experiences during the socialisation period, can manifest itself in fear and aggression as the dog grows up. Your puppy needs lots of positive interaction, which of course includes human contact, affection, handling and exposure to other animals.

Once your pup has received his necessary vaccinations, feel

FEEDING TIPS

You will probably start feeding your pup the same food that he has been getting from the breeder; the breeder should give you a few days' supply to start you off. Although you should not give your pup too many treats, you will want to have puppy treats on hand for coaxing, training, rewards, etc. Be careful, though, as a small pup's calorie requirements are relatively low and a few treats can add up to almost a full day's worth of calories without the required nutrition.

free to take him out and about (on his lead, of course). Walk him around the neighbourhood, take him on your daily errands, let people pet him, let him meet other dogs and pets, etc. Puppies do not have to try to make friends; there will be no shortage of people who will want to introduce themselves. Just make sure that you carefully supervise each meeting. If the neighbour-hood children want to say hello, for example, that is great—children and pups most often make great companions. However, sometimes an excited child can unintentionally handle a pup too roughly, or an overzealous pup can playfully nip a little too hard. You want to make socialisation experiences positive ones. What a pup learns during this very formative stage will affect his

MEET THE WORLD

Thorough socialisation includes not only meeting new people but also being introduced to new experiences such as riding in the car, having his coat brushed, hearing the television, walking in a crowd—the list is endless. The more your pup experiences, and the more positive the experiences are, the less of a shock and the less frightening it will be for your pup to encounter new things.

A FORTNIGHT'S GRACE
It will take at least two weeks for your puppy to become accustomed to his new surroundings. Give him lots of love, attention, handling, frequent opportunities to relieve himself, a diet he likes to eat and a place he can call his own.

attitude toward future encounters. You want your dog to be comfortable around everyone. A pup that has a bad experience with a child may grow up to be a dog that is shy around or aggressive toward children.

CONSISTENCY IN TRAINING
Dogs, being pack animals, naturally need a leader, or else they try to establish dominance in their packs. When you welcome a dog into your family, the choice of who becomes the leader and who becomes the 'pack' is entirely up to you! Your pup's intuitive quest for dominance, coupled with the

fact that it is nearly impossible to look at an adorable Curly pup with his 'puppy-dog' eyes and not cave in, give the pup almost an unfair advantage in getting the upper hand! A pup will definitely test the waters to see what he can and cannot do. Do not give in to those pleading eyes—stand your ground when it comes to disciplining the pup and make sure that all family members do the same. It will only confuse the pup if Mother tells him to get off the sofa when he is used to sitting up there with Father to watch the nightly news. Avoid discrepancies by having all members of the household decide on the rules before the pup even comes home…and be consistent in enforcing them! Early training shapes the dog's personality, so you cannot be unclear in what you expect.

COMMON PUPPY PROBLEMS
The best way to prevent puppy problems is to be proactive in

QUALITY FOOD
The cost of food must be mentioned. All dogs need a good-quality food with an adequate supply of protein to develop their bones and muscles properly. Most dogs are not picky eaters but, unless fed properly, can quickly succumb to skin problems.

stopping an undesirable behaviour as soon as it starts. The old saying 'You can't teach an old dog new tricks' does not necessarily hold true, but it is true that it is much easier to discourage bad behaviour in a young developing pup than to wait until the pup's bad behaviour becomes the adult dog's bad habit. There are some problems that are especially prevalent in puppies as they develop.

NIPPING

As puppies start to teethe, they feel the need to sink their teeth into anything available...unfortunately, that usually includes your fingers, arms, hair and toes. You may find this behaviour cute for the first five seconds...until you feel just how sharp those puppy teeth are. Nipping is something you want to discourage immediately and consistently with a firm 'No!' (or whatever number of firm 'Nos' it takes for him to understand that you mean business). Then, replace your finger with an appropriate chew toy. While this behaviour is merely annoying when the dog is young, it can become dangerous as your Curly Coated Retriever's adult teeth grow in and his jaws develop, and he continues to think it is okay to gnaw on human appendages. Your Curly does not mean any harm with a friendly nip, but he also does not know his own strength.

CRYING/WHINING

Your pup will often cry, whine, whimper, howl or make some type of commotion when he is left alone. This is basically his way of calling out for attention to make sure that you know he is there and that you have not forgotten

PROPER SOCIALISATION
The socialisation period for puppies is from age 8 to 16 weeks. This is the time when puppies need to leave their birth family and take up residence with their new owners, where they will meet many new people, other pets, etc. Failure to be adequately socialised can cause the dog to grow up fearing others and being shy and unfriendly due to a lack of self-confidence.

CHEWING TIPS

Chewing goes hand in hand with nipping in the sense that a teething puppy is always looking for a way to soothe his aching gums. In this case, instead of chewing on you, he may have taken a liking to your favourite shoe or something else which he should not be chewing. Again, realise that this is a normal canine behaviour that does not need to be discouraged, only redirected. Your pup just needs to be taught what is acceptable to chew on and what is off limits. Consistently tell him NO when you catch him chewing on something forbidden and give him a chew toy. Conversely, praise him when you catch him chewing on something appropriate. In this way you are discouraging the inappropriate behaviour and reinforcing the desired behaviour. The puppy chewing should stop after his adult teeth have come in, but an adult dog continues to chew for various reasons—perhaps because he is bored, perhaps to relieve tension or perhaps he just likes to chew. That is why it is important to redirect his chewing when he is still young.

about him. Your puppy feels insecure when he is left alone, when you are out of the house and he is in his crate or when you are in another part of the house and he cannot see you. The noise he is making is an expression of the anxiety he feels at being alone, so he needs to be taught that being alone is okay. You are not actually training the dog to stop making noise; rather, you are training him to feel comfortable when he is alone and thus removing the need for him to make the noise. This is where the crate with cosy bedding and a toy comes in handy. You want to know that your pup is safe when you are not there to supervise, and you know that he will be safe in his crate rather than roaming freely about the house.

In order for the pup to stay in his crate without making a fuss, he first needs to be comfortable in his crate. On that note, it is extremely important that the crate is never used as a form of

PUPPY PROBLEMS

The majority of problems that are commonly seen in young pups will disappear as your dog gets older. However, how you deal with problems when he is young will determine how he reacts to discipline as an adult dog. It is important to establish who is boss (hopefully it will be you!) right away when you are first bonding with your dog. This bond will set the tone for the rest of your life together.

place of his own for safety and retreat.

Accustom the pup to the crate in short, gradually increasing time intervals in which you put him in the crate, maybe with a treat, and stay in the room with him. If he cries or makes a fuss, do not go to him, but stay in his sight. Gradually he will realise that staying in his crate is all right without your help, and it will not be so traumatic for him when you are not around. You may want to leave the radio on softly when you leave the house; the sound of human voices may be comforting to him.

YOUR SCHEDULE . . .

If you lead an erratic, unpredictable life, with daily or weekly changes in your work requirements, consider the problems of owning a puppy. The new puppy has to be fed regularly, socialised (loved, petted, handled, introduced to other people) and, most importantly, allowed to visit outdoors for toilet training. As the dog gets older, it can be more tolerant of deviations in its feeding and toilet relief.

punishment; this will cause the pup to view the crate as a negative place, rather than as a

Chewing is every puppy's favourite game. Discourage biting games immediately or you will have an unruly adult to contend with.

The Curly puppy will fit into your home environment quite naturally. Be certain you have everything you need before the puppy arrives home.

DIETARY AND FEEDING CONSIDERATIONS

Today the choices of food for your Curly are many and varied. There are simply dozens of brands of food in all sorts of flavours and textures, ranging from puppy diets to those for seniors. There are even hypoallergenic and low-calorie diets available. Because your Curly's food has a bearing on coat, health and temperament, it is essential that the most suitable diet is selected for a Curly of his age. It is fair to say, however, that even experienced owners can be perplexed by the enormous range of foods available. Only understanding what is best for your dog will help you reach an informed decision.

Dog foods are produced in three basic types: dried, semi-moist and tinned. Dried foods are useful for the cost-conscious, for overall they tend to be less expensive than semi-moist or

Training ensures your Curly's safety as well as good manners. Learning to come when called is essential for all dogs.

tinned foods. Dried foods also contain the least fat and the most preservatives. In general, tinned foods are made up of 60–70 percent water, while semi-moist ones often contain so much sugar that they are perhaps the least preferred by owners, even though their dogs seem to like them.

When selecting your dog's diet, three stages of development must be considered: the puppy stage, the adult stage and the senior or veteran stage.

Puppy Stage

Puppies instinctively want to suck milk from their mother's teats; a

FOOD PREFERENCE

Selecting the best dried dog food is difficult. There is no majority consensus among veterinary scientists as to the value of nutrient analyses (protein, fat, fibre, moisture, ash, cholesterol, minerals, etc.). All agree that feeding trials are what matter, but you also have to consider the individual dog. The dog's weight, age and activity level, and what pleases his taste, all must be considered. It is probably best to take the advice of your veterinary surgeon. Every dog's dietary require-ments vary, even during the lifetime of a particular dog.

If your dog is fed a good dried food, it does not require supple-ments of meat or vegetables. Dogs do appreciate a little variety in their diets, so you may choose to stay with the same brand but vary the flavour. Alternatively, you may wish to add a little flavoured stock to give a difference to the taste.

normal puppy will exhibit this behaviour just a few moments following birth. If puppies do not attempt to suckle within the first half-hour or so, they should be encouraged to do so by placing them on the nipples, having selected ones with plenty of milk. This early milk supply is important in providing the essential colostrum, which protects the puppies during the first eight to ten weeks of their lives. Although a mother's milk is much better than any milk formula, despite there being some excellent ones available, if the puppies do not feed, the breeder will have to feed them by hand. For those with less experience, advice from a veterinary surgeon is important so that not only the right quantity of milk is fed but also that of correct quality, fed at suitably frequent intervals, usually every two hours during the first few days of life.

Puppies should be allowed to nurse from their mothers for about the first six weeks, although, starting around the third or fourth week, the breeder will begin to introduce small portions of suitable solid food. Most breeders like to introduce alternate milk and meat meals initially, building up to weaning time.

By the time the puppies are seven or a maximum of eight weeks old, they should be fully weaned and fed solely on a proprietary puppy food. Selection of the most suitable, good-quality diet at this time is essential, for a puppy's fastest growth rate is during the first year of life. Veterinary surgeons are usually able to offer advice in this regard and, although the frequency of meals will be reduced over time, only when a young dog has reached the age of about 12 months should an adult diet be fed. Puppy and junior diets should be well balanced for the needs of your dog so that, except in certain circumstances, additional vitamins, minerals and proteins will not be required.

FEEDING TIP

You must store your dried dog food carefully. Open packages of dog food quickly lose their vitamin value, usually within 90 days of being opened. Mould spores and vermin could also contaminate the food.

ADULT DIETS

A dog is considered an adult when it has stopped growing, which in the slow-maturing Curly Coated Retriever is not until around three to four years of age. However, the diet of a Curly can be changed to an adult one at about 12 months of age. Again you should rely upon your veterinary surgeon or dietary specialist to recommend an acceptable maintenance diet. Major dog food manufacturers specialise in this type of food, and it is merely necessary for you to select the one best suited to your dog's needs. Active dogs have different requirements than sedate dogs.

SENIOR DIETS

As dogs get older, their metabolism changes. The older dog usually exercises less, moves more slowly and sleeps more. This change in lifestyle and physiological performance requires a change in diet. Since these changes take place slowly, they might not be recognisable. What is easily recognisable is weight gain. By continuing to feed your dog an adult-maintenance diet when it is slowing down metabolically, your dog will gain weight. Obesity in an older dog compounds the health problems that already accompany old age.

As your dog gets older, few of his organs function up to par. The kidneys slow down and the

FEEDING TIPS

Dog food must be at room tempera-ture, neither too hot nor too cold. Fresh water, changed daily and served in a clean bowl, is mandatory, especially when feeding dried food.

Never feed your dog from the table while you are eating, and never feed your dog leftovers from your own meal. They usually contain too much fat and too much seasoning.

Dogs must chew their food. Hard pellets are excellent; soups and slurries are to be avoided.

Don't add leftovers or any extras to normal dog food. The normal food is usually balanced, and adding something extra destroys the balance.

Except for age-related changes, dogs do not require dietary variations. They can be fed the same diet, day after day, without becoming ill.

intestines become less efficient. These age-related factors are best handled with a change in diet and a change in feeding schedule to give smaller portions that are more easily digested. There is no single best diet for every older dog. While many dogs do well on light or senior diets, other dogs do better on puppy diets or other special premium diets such as lamb and rice. Be sensitive to your senior Curly's diet, as this will help control other problems that may arise with your old friend. Depending on the individual dog's metabolism, activity level and lifestyle, Curlies usually switch to senior diets around seven or eight years of age.

WATER

Just as your dog needs proper nutrition from his food, water is an essential 'nutrient' as well. Water keeps the dog's body properly hydrated and promotes normal function of the body's systems. During house-training it is necessary to keep an eye on how much water your Curly is drinking, but once he is reliably trained he should have access to clean fresh water at all times, especially if you feed dried food. Make certain that the dog's water bowl is clean, and change the water often.

EXERCISE

All dogs require some form of exercise, regardless of breed. A sedentary lifestyle is as harmful to a dog as it is to a person. The Curly is definitely an active breed that enjoys exercise, but you don't have to be an Olympic athlete to provide your dog with a sufficient amount of activity! Exercising your Curly can be enjoyable and healthy for both of you. Brisk walks will stimulate heart rates and build muscle for both dog and owner. As the dog reaches adulthood, the speed and distance of the walks can be increased as long as they are both kept reasonable and comfortable for both of you. Keep in mind that a Curly puppy should not engage in jumping or high-impact exercise before one year of age to prevent causing stress to his developing joints.

Play sessions in the garden and letting the dog run free in the garden under your supervision also are sufficient forms of exercise for the Curly Coated Retriever. Fetching games can be played indoors or out; these are excellent for giving your dog active play that he will enjoy

DO DOGS HAVE TASTE BUDS?

Watching a dog 'wolf' or gobble his food, seemingly without chewing, leads an owner to wonder whether their dogs can taste anything. Yes, dogs have taste buds, with sensory perception of sweet, salty and sour. Puppies are born with fully mature taste buds.

DRINK, DRANK, DRUNK— MAKE IT A DOUBLE

In both humans and dogs, as well as most living organisms, water forms the major part of nearly every body tissue. Naturally, we take water for granted, but without it, life as we know it would cease.

For dogs, water is needed to keep their bodies functioning biochemically. Additionally, water is needed to replace the water lost while panting. Unlike humans, who are able to sweat to dissipate heat, dogs must pant to cool down, thereby losing the vital water from their bodies needed to regulate their body temperatures. Humans lose electrolyte-containing products and other body-fluid components through sweating; dogs do not lose anything except water.

Water is essential always, but especially so when the weather is hot or humid or when your dog is exercising or working vigorously.

What are you feeding your dog?

Read the label on your dog food. Many dog foods only advise what 50—55% of the contents are, leaving the other 45% in doubt.

Calcium 1.3%
Fatty Acids 1.6%
Crude Fibre 4.6%
Moisture 11%
Crude Fat 14%
Crude Protein 22%
45.5% ? ? ?

while engaging in something that comes naturally to him— retrieving! When your Curly runs after the ball or object, praise him for picking it up and encourage him to bring it back to you for another throw. Never go to the object and pick it up yourself, or you'll soon find that you are the one retrieving the objects rather than the dog! Remember, for outdoor play, you must have a securely fenced-in garden. You want your Curly to run, but not run away!

Swimming is also an excellent form of exercise for a water breed like the Curly Coated Retriever. They naturally take to water and are very talented swimmers. You will need to ensure that the swimming area is safe, but once you've found an appropriate

'DOES THIS COLLAR MAKE ME LOOK FAT?'

While humans may obsess about how they look and how trim their bodies are, many people believe that extra weight on their dogs is a good thing. The truth is, pets should not be over- or under-weight, as both can lead to or signal sickness. In order to tell how fit your pet is, run your hands over his ribs. Are his ribs buried under a layer of fat or are they sticking out considerably? If your pet is within his normal weight range, you should be able to feel the ribs easily, but they should not protrude abnormally. If you stand above him, the outline of his body should resemble an hourglass. Some breeds do tend to be leaner while some are a bit stockier, but making sure your dog is the right weight for his breed will certainly contribute to his good health.

CHANGE IN DIET

As your dog's caretaker, you know the importance of keeping his diet consistent, but sometimes when you run out of food or if you're on holiday, you have to make a change quickly. Some dogs will experience digestive problems, but most will not. If you are planning on changing your dog's menu, do so gradually to ensure that your dog will not have any problems. Over a period of four to five days, slowly add some new food to your dog's old food, increasing the percentage of new food each day.

place, your Curly will not need convincing to jump right in! Of course, puppies should be introduced to water slowly, but it will not take them long to become confident in the water.

Bear in mind that an overweight dog should never be suddenly over-exercised; instead he should be encouraged to increase exercise slowly. Not only is exercise essential to keep the dog's body fit, it is essential to his mental well-being. A bored dog will find something to do, which

Your local pet
shop will have
the tools
necessary to
properly groom
your Curly. Very
little grooming is
necessary.
Brushing should
be done only
twice a year.

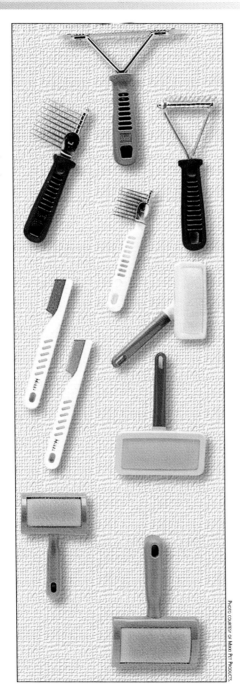

often manifests itself in some type of destructive behaviour. In this sense, exercise is essential for the owner's mental well-being as well!

GROOMING

ROUTINE CARE

The Curly could easily be called a wash-and-wear dog because of its easy-care, tightly curled coat. Daily care is unnecessary; the coat should never be brushed or combed out, since that would stretch and frizz the coat. Brushing is necessary only twice a year during heavy shedding periods in spring and fall. A slight bit of routine shedding does occur, however, when the hair shaft stops growing, dies and

GROOMING EQUIPMENT

How much grooming equipment you purchase will depend on how much grooming you are going to do. Here are some basics:

- Natural bristle brush
- Slicker brush
- Metal comb
- Scissors
- Blaster
- Rubber mat
- Dog shampoo
- Spray hose attachment
- Ear cleaner
- Cotton wipes
- Towels
- Nail clippers

eventually falls out.

Most owners keep their Curlies groomed with regular bathing, at least three or four times a year, which helps to control normal coat loss and keeps the dog clean and tidy. The curly coat is frequently oily, which tends to attract and accumulate dead hair and dirt. Bathing removes the dust and allergens from the coat, which is important for Curly owners who are allergic to such things.

Frequent swimming sessions will also aid in removing dust accumulation from the coat. Hunters rarely bath their Curlies during hunting season so that the coat will retain its natural oil and thus provide more protection from the elements. All hunting dogs should be checked after each hunting session for burrs and other debris that may have lodged in the coat during field work.

Although the breed standard does not require extensive grooming for the show ring, most judges expect the dogs to be trimmed before entering the show ring. Exhibitors usually scissor excess hair from the tail, ears and legs.

BATHING

Dogs do not need to be bathed as often as humans, but regular bathing is essential for healthy skin and a healthy, shiny coat. Again, like most anything, if you

The dog's coat should be sprayed with water prior to grooming.

A fine-toothed wire comb is useful for monitoring for parasites and removing any debris from the coat.

Trimming is necessary for a show dog, to remove any straggly hairs and tidy up the Curly's appearance.

made for dogs. Do not use a product made for human hair. Work the shampoo all the way down to the skin. You can use this opportunity to check the skin for any bumps, bites or other abnormalities. Do not neglect any area of the body—get all of the hard-to-reach places.

Once the dog has been thoroughly shampooed, he requires an equally thorough rinsing. Shampoo left in the coat can be irritating to the dog's skin. Protect his eyes from the shampoo by shielding them with your hand and directing the flow of water in the opposite direction. You should also avoid getting water in the ear canal. Be prepared for your dog to shake out his coat— you might want to stand back, but make sure you have a hold on the

accustom your pup to being bathed as a puppy, it will be second nature by the time he grows up. With the Curly, anything involving water is first nature, and Curly puppies take little coaxing to enjoy time in the bath—limiting the fun is the usual challenge.

Make certain that your dog has a good non-slip surface on which to stand. Begin by wetting the dog's coat, checking the water temperature to make sure that it is neither too hot nor too cold. A shower or hose attachment is necessary for thoroughly wetting and rinsing the coat.

Next, apply shampoo to the dog's coat and work it into a good lather. Wash the head last, as you do not want shampoo to drip into the dog's eyes while you are washing the rest of his body. You should use only a shampoo that is

Curlies are easy to bath! Use a sponge, plenty of soap and room-temperature water.

dog to keep him from running through the house.

EAR CLEANING

The ears should be kept clean with a cotton wipe and ear powder made especially for dogs. Do not probe into the ear canal with a cotton bud, as this can cause injury. Be on the lookout for any signs of infection or ear mite infestation. If your Curly has been shaking his head or scratching at his ears frequently, this usually indicates a problem. If the dog's ears have an unusual odour, this is a sure sign of mite infestation or infection, and a signal to have his ears checked by the veterinary surgeon.

Curlies who swim frequently should have their ears checked and cleaned every day to prevent fungus growth and other ear problems from occurring. Regular use of an ear cleanser will also keep excess ear wax from accumulating.

NAIL CLIPPING

Your Curly should be accustomed to having his nails trimmed at an early age since nail clipping will be part of your maintenance routine throughout his life. Not only does it look nicer, but long nails can scratch someone unintentionally. Also, a long nail has a better chance of ripping and bleeding, or causing the feet to spread. A good rule of thumb is that if you can hear your dog's

Since the coat is water-proof, be sure to work the water in with a sponge and to thoroughly rinse the coat to remove any soap residue.

BATHING BEAUTY

Once you are sure that the dog is thoroughly rinsed, squeeze the excess water out of his coat with your hand and dry him with a heavy towel. You may choose to use a blaster on his coat or just let it dry naturally. In cold weather, never allow your dog outside with a wet coat.

There are 'dry bath' products on the market, which are sprays and powders intended for spot cleaning, that can be used between regular baths if necessary. They are not substitutes for regular baths, but they are easy to use for touch-ups as they do not require rinsing.

Clean the ears with ear powder and a soft cotton wipe.

Most dogs do not enjoy having the nails clipped. Purchase a top-quality, guillotine-style clipper to make the task easier for you and your Curly.

The areas around the eyes can be cleaned with a cotton wipe and cleansing solution made for the task.

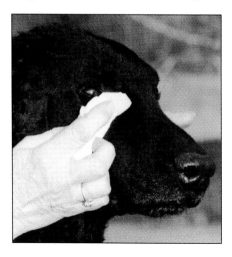

Keep some type of clotting agent on hand, such as a styptic pencil or styptic powder (the type used for shaving). This will stop the bleeding quickly when applied to the end of the cut nail. Do not panic if you cut the quick, just stop the bleeding and talk soothingly to your dog. Once he has calmed down, move on to the next nail. It is better to clip a little

nails clicking on the floor when he walks, his nails are too long.

Before you start cutting, make sure you can identify the 'quick' in each nail. The quick is a blood vessel that runs through the centre of each nail and grows rather close to the end. The quick will bleed if accidentally cut, which will be quite painful for the dog as it contains nerve endings.

NAIL FILING

You can purchase an electric tool to grind down a dog's nails rather than cut them. Some dogs don't seem to mind the electric grinder but will object strongly to nail clippers. Talking it over with your veterinary surgeon will help you make the right choice.

at a time, particularly with black-nailed dogs.

Hold your pup steady as you begin trimming his nails; you do not want him to make any sudden movements or run away. Talk to him soothingly and stroke him as

PEDICURE TIP

A dog that spends a lot of time outside on a hard surface, such as cement or pavement, will have his nails naturally worn down and may not need to have them trimmed as often, except maybe in the colder months when he is not outside as much. Regardless, it is best to get your dog accustomed to the nail-trimming procedure at an early age so that he is used to it. Some dogs are especially sensitive about having their feet touched, but if a dog has experienced it since puppyhood, it should not bother him.

Nail Maintenance

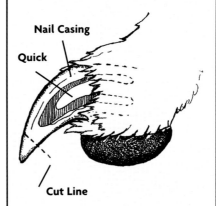

Nail Casing

Quick

Cut Line

Dark-Coloured Nails

With black or dark nails, it's best to clip only the tip of the nail or to use a file.

Light-Coloured Nails

In light-coloured nails, clipping is much simpler because you can see the vein (or quick) that grows inside the casing.

SAFE TRAVELS

The most extensive travel you do with your dog may be limited to trips to the veterinary surgeon's office—or you may decide to bring him along for long distances when the family goes on holiday. Whichever the case, it is important to consider your dog's safety while travelling.

you clip. Holding his foot in your hand, simply take off the end of each nail with one swift clip. You should purchase nail clippers that are made for use on dogs; you can probably find them wherever you buy pet or grooming supplies.

TRAVELLING WITH YOUR DOG

CAR TRAVEL

You should accustom your Curly to riding in a car at an early age. You may or may not take him in

ON THE ROAD

If you are going on a long motor trip with your dog, be sure the hotels are dog-friendly. Many hotels do not accept dogs. Also take along some ice that can be thawed and offered to your dog if he becomes overheated. Most dogs like to lick ice.

the car often, but at the very least he will need to go to the vet and you do not want these trips to be traumatic for the dog or troublesome for you. The safest way for a dog to ride in the car is in his crate. If he uses a crate in the house, you can use the same crate for travel.

Put the pup in the crate and see how he reacts. If he seems uneasy, you can have a passenger hold him on his lap while you drive. Another option for car travel is a specially made safety harness for dogs, which straps the dog in much like a seat belt. Do not let the dog roam loose in the

HEAT STROKE

Never leave your dog alone in the car. In hot weather, your dog can die from the high temperature inside a closed vehicle; even a car parked in the shade can heat up very quickly. Leaving the window open is dangerous as well since the dog can hurt himself trying to get out.

Air Travel

While it is possible to take a dog on a flight within Britain, this is fairly unusual and advance permission is always required. The dog will be required to travel in a fibreglass crate and you should always check in advance with the airline regarding specific requirements. To help put the dog at ease, give him one of his favourite toys in the crate. Do not feed the dog for at least six hours before the trip in order to minimise his need to relieve

vehicle—this is very dangerous! If you should stop short, your dog can be thrown and injured. If the dog starts climbing on you and pestering you while you are driving, you will not be able to concentrate on the road. It is an unsafe situation for everyone— human and canine.

For long trips, be prepared to stop to let the dog relieve himself. Take with you whatever you need to clean up after him, including some paper kitchen towels and perhaps some old towelling for use should he have a toileting accident in the car or suffer from travel sickness.

LEAD, LEAD, LEAD

When travelling, never let your dog off-lead in a strange area. Your dog could run away out of fear, decide to chase a passing squirrel or cat or simply want to stretch his legs without restriction—if any of these happen, you might never see your canine friend again.

himself. However, certain regulations specify that water must always be made available to the dog in the crate.

Make sure your dog is properly identified and that your contact information appears on his ID tags and on his crate. Animals travel in a different area of the plane than human passengers, so every rule must be strictly followed to prevent the risk of getting separated from your dog.

BOARDING

So you want to take a family holiday—and you want to include *all* members of the

family. You would probably make arrangements for accommodation ahead of time anyway, but this is especially important when travelling with a dog. You do not want to make an overnight stop at the only place around for miles, only to find out that they do not allow dogs. Also, you do not want to reserve a place for your family without confirming that you are travelling with a dog, because, if it is against their policy, you may end up without a place to stay.

Alternatively, if you are travelling and choose not to bring your Curly, you will have to make arrangements for him while you are away. Some options are to take him to a neighbour's house to stay while you are gone, to have a trusted neighbour pop in often or stay at your house or to bring your dog to a reputable boarding kennel. If you choose to board him at a kennel, you should visit in advance to see the facilities provided and where the dogs are kept. Are the dogs' areas spacious and kept clean? Talk to some of the employees and observe how they treat the dogs—do they spend time with the dogs, play with them,

Every dog should have an identification tag securely attached to his everyday collar.

exercise them, etc.? Also find out the kennel's policy on vaccinations and what they require. This is for all of the dogs' safety, since there is a greater risk of diseases being passed from dog to dog when dogs are kept together.

IDENTIFICATION
Your Curly is your valued companion and friend. That is why you always keep a close eye on him and you have made sure that he cannot escape from the garden or wriggle out of his collar and run away from you. However, accidents can happen and there may come a time when your dog unexpectedly becomes separated from you. If this unfortunate event should occur, the first thing on your mind will be finding him. Proper identification, including an ID tag, a tattoo and possibly a microchip, will increase the chances of his being returned to you safely and quickly.

COLLAR REQUIRED
If your dog gets lost, he is not able to ask for directions home. Identification tags fastened to the collar give important information— the dog's name, the owner's name, the owner's address and a telephone number where the owner can be reached. This makes it easy for whomever finds the dog to contact the owner and arrange to have the dog returned. An added advantage is that a person will be more likely to approach a lost dog who has ID tags on his collar; it tells the person that this is somebody's pet rather than a stray. This is the easiest and fastest method of identification, provided that the tags stay on the collar and the collar stays on the dog.

The Curly Coated Retriever learns quickly but bores just as easily.

A natural retriever, the Curly responds instinctively to training for hunting tasks.

Living with an untrained dog is a lot like owning a piano that you do not know how to play—it is a nice object to look at but it does not do much more than that to bring you pleasure. Now try taking piano lessons, and suddenly the piano comes alive and brings forth magical sounds and rhythms that set your heart singing and your body swaying.

The same is true with your Curly Coated Retriever. Any dog is a big responsibility and, if not trained sensibly, may develop unacceptable behaviour that annoys you or could even cause family friction.

To train your Curly, you may like to enrol in an obedience class. Teach your dog good manners as you learn how and why he behaves the way he does. Find out how to communicate with your dog and how to recognise and understand his communications with you. Suddenly the dog takes on a new role in your life—he is clever, interesting, well behaved and fun to be with. He demonstrates his bond of devotion to you daily. In other words, your Curly Coated Retriever does wonders for your ego because he constantly reminds you that you are not only his leader, you are his hero!

Those involved with teaching dog obedience and counselling owners about their dogs' behaviour have discovered some interesting facts about dog

REAP THE REWARDS

If you start with a normal, healthy dog and give him time, patience and some carefully executed lessons, you will reap the rewards of that training for the life of the dog. And what a life it will be! The two of you will find immeasurable pleasure in the companionship you have built together with love, respect and understanding.

ownership. For example, training dogs when they are puppies results in the highest rate of success in developing well-mannered and well-adjusted adult dogs. Training an older dog, from six months to six years of age, can produce almost equal results providing that the owner accepts the dog's slower rate of learning capability and is willing to work patiently to help the dog succeed at developing to his fullest potential. Unfortunately, many owners of untrained adult dogs lack the patience factor, so they do not persist until their dogs are successful at learning particular behaviours.

Training a puppy aged 10 to 16 weeks (20 weeks at the most) is like working with a dry sponge in a pool of water. The pup soaks up whatever you show him and constantly looks for more things to do and learn. At this early age, his body is not yet producing hormones, and therein lies the reason for such a high rate of success. Without hormones, the pup is focused on his owners and not particularly interested in investigating other places, dogs, people, etc. You are his leader: his provider of food, water, shelter and security. He latches onto you and wants to stay close. He will usually follow you from room to room, will not let you out of his sight when you are outdoors with him and will respond in like manner to the people and animals you encounter. If you greet a friend warmly, he will be happy to greet the person as well. If, however, you are hesitant or anxious about the approach of a stranger, he will respond accordingly.

Once the puppy begins to produce hormones, his natural curiosity emerges and he begins to investigate the world around him. It is at this time when you may notice that the untrained dog begins to wander away from you and even ignore your commands to stay close. When this behaviour becomes a problem, you have two choices: get rid of the dog or train him. It is strongly urged that you choose the latter option and read on.

You usually will be able to find obedience classes within a reasonable distance from your home, but you can also do a lot to train your dog yourself. Sometimes there are classes available, but the tuition is too costly. Whatever the circumstances, the solution to training your dog without obedience

Adults and puppies both respond to training, and, of course, to a tasty treat as a reward!

classes lies within the pages of this book.

This chapter is devoted to helping you train your Curly Coated Retriever at home. If the recommended procedures are followed faithfully, you may expect positive results that will prove rewarding both to you and your dog.

Whether your new charge is a puppy or a mature adult, the methods of teaching and the techniques we use in training basic behaviours are the same. After all, no Curly, and any other dog, for that matter, whether puppy or adult, likes harsh or

THE HAND THAT FEEDS

To a dog's way of thinking, your hands are like his mouth in terms of a defence mechanism. If you squeeze him too tightly, he might just bite you because that would be his normal response. This is not aggressive biting and, although all biting should be discouraged, you need the discipline in learning how to handle your dog.

PARENTAL GUIDANCE

Training a dog is a life experience. Many parents admit that much of what they know about raising children they learned from caring for their dogs. Dogs respond to love, fairness and guidance, just as children do. Become a good dog owner and you may become an even better parent.

inhumane methods. All creatures, however, respond favourably to gentle motivational methods and sincere praise and encouragement. Now let us get started.

HOUSE-TRAINING

You can train a puppy to relieve himself wherever you choose, but this must be somewhere suitable. You should bear in mind from the outset that when your puppy is old enough to go out in public

Mischief and the Curly pup go hand-in-hand! Patience and a sense of humour are keys to training success.

places, any canine deposits must be removed at once. You will always have to carry with you a small plastic bag or 'poop-scoop.'

Outdoor training includes such surfaces as grass, soil and cement. Indoor training usually means training your dog to newspaper. When deciding on the surface and location that you will want your Curly to use, be sure it is going to be permanent. Training your dog to grass and then changing your mind a few months later is extremely difficult for both dog and owner.

Next, choose the command you will use each and every time you want your puppy to void. 'Hurry up' and 'Toilet' are examples of commands commonly used by dog owners. Get in the habit of giving the puppy your chosen relief command before you take him out. That way, when he becomes an adult, you will be able to determine if he wants to go out when you ask him. A confirmation will be signs of interest, wagging his tail, watching you intently, going to the door, etc.

PUPPY'S NEEDS

Puppy needs to relieve himself after play periods, after each meal, after he has been sleeping and at any time he indicates that he is looking for a place to urinate or defecate. The urinary and intestinal tract muscles of very young puppies are not fully developed. Therefore, like human babies, puppies need to relieve themselves frequently.

Take your puppy out often—every hour for an eight-week-old, for example—and always immediately after sleeping and eating. The older the puppy, the less often he will need to relieve himself. Finally, as a mature healthy adult, he will require only three to five relief trips per day.

HOUSING

Since the types of housing and control you provide for your puppy have a direct relationship on the success of house-training, we consider the various aspects of both before we begin training.

Taking a new puppy home and turning him loose in your house can be compared to turning a child loose in a sports arena and telling the child that the place is all his! The sheer enormity of the place would be too much for him to handle. Instead, offer the puppy clearly defined areas where he can play, sleep, eat and live. A room of the house where the family gathers is the most obvious choice. Puppies are social animals and need to feel a part of the pack right from the start. Hearing your voice, watching you while you are doing things and smelling you nearby are all positive reinforcers that he is now a member of your pack. Usually a family room, the

TRAINING TIP
Dogs will do anything for your attention. If you reward the dog when he is calm and resting, you will develop a well-mannered dog. If, on the other hand, you greet your dog excitedly and encourage him to wrestle with you, the dog will greet you the same way and you will have a hyperactive dog on your hands.

Secure in his wire crate, this Curly pup is safe and out of trouble—yet still involved in the family fun.

kitchen or a nearby adjoining breakfast area is ideal for providing safety and security for both puppy and owner.

Within the designated room, there should be a smaller area that the puppy can call his own. An alcove, a wire or fibreglass dog crate or a fenced (not boarded!)

PAPER CAPER

Never line your pup's sleeping area with newspaper. Puppy litters are usually raised on newspaper and, once in your home, the puppy will immediately associate newspaper with voiding. Never put newspaper on any floor while house-training, as this will only confuse the puppy. If you are paper-training him, use paper in his designated relief area ONLY. Finally, restrict water intake after evening meals. Offer a few licks at a time—never let a young puppy gulp water after meals.

corner from which he can view the activities of his new family will be fine. The size of the area or crate is the key factor here. The area must be large enough so that the puppy can lie down and stretch out, as well as stand up, without rubbing his head on the top. At the same time, it must be small enough so that he cannot relieve himself at one end and sleep at the other without coming into contact with his droppings before he is fully trained to relieve himself outside. Dogs are, by nature, clean animals and will not remain close to their relief areas unless forced to do so. In those cases, they then become dirty dogs and usually remain that way for life.

The dog's designated area should contain clean bedding and a toy. Water must always be available, in a non-spill container.

CONTROL
By control, we mean helping the puppy to create a lifestyle pattern that will be compatible to that of his human pack (YOU!). Just as we guide little children to learn our way of life, we must show the puppy when it is time to play, eat, sleep, exercise and even entertain himself.

Your puppy should always sleep in his crate. He should also learn that, during times of household confusion and excessive human activity, such as

CANINE DEVELOPMENT SCHEDULE

It is important to understand how and at what age a puppy develops into adulthood. If you are a puppy owner, consult the following Canine Development Schedule to determine the stage of development your puppy is currently experiencing. This knowledge will help you as you work with the puppy in the weeks and months ahead.

Period	Age	Characteristics
FIRST TO THIRD	**BIRTH TO SEVEN WEEKS**	Puppy needs food, sleep and warmth, and responds to simple and gentle touching. Needs mother for security and disciplining. Needs littermates for learning and interacting with other dogs. Pup learns to function within a pack and learns pack order of dominance. Begin socialising with adults and children for short periods. Begins to become aware of its environment.
FOURTH	**EIGHT TO TWELVE WEEKS**	Brain is fully developed. Needs socialising with outside world. Remove from mother and littermates. Needs to change from canine pack to human pack. Human dominance necessary. Fear period occurs between 8 and 12 weeks. Avoid fright and pain.
FIFTH	**THIRTEEN TO SIXTEEN WEEKS**	Training and formal obedience should begin. Less association with other dogs, more with people, places, situations. Period will pass easily if you remember this is pup's change-to-adolescence time. Be firm and fair. Flight instinct prominent. Permissiveness and over-disciplining can do permanent damage. Praise for good behaviour.
JUVENILE	**FOUR TO EIGHT MONTHS**	Another fear period about 7 to 8 months of age. It passes quickly, but be cautious of fright and pain. Sexual maturity reached. Dominant traits established. Dog should understand sit, down, come and stay by now.

NOTE: THESE ARE APPROXIMATE TIME FRAMES. ALLOW FOR INDIVIDUAL DIFFERENCES IN PUPPIES.

A well-trained
Curly is easier to
manage in every
situation.
Travelling with a
trained dog can
be a pleasure for
everyone
involved.

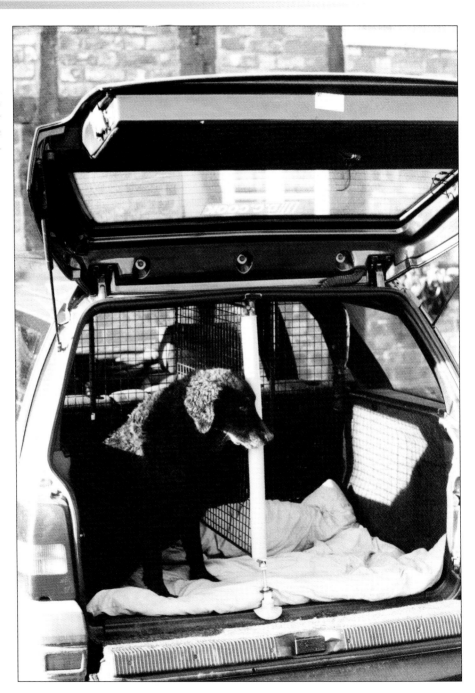

HONOUR AND OBEY
Dogs are the most honourable animals in existence. They consider another species (humans) as their own. They interface with you. You are their leader. Puppies perceive children to be on their level; their actions around small children are different from their behaviour around their adult masters.

at breakfast when family members are preparing for the day, he can play by himself in relative safety and comfort in his designated area. Each time you leave the puppy alone, he should understand exactly where he is to stay.

Puppies are chewers. They cannot tell the difference between lamp cords, television wires, shoes, table legs, etc. Chewing into a television wire, for example, can be fatal to the puppy while a shorted wire can start a fire in the house. If the puppy chews on the arm of the chair when he is alone, you will probably discipline him angrily when you get home. Thus, he makes the association that your coming home means he is going to be punished. (He will not remember chewing the chair and is incapable of making the association of the discipline with his naughty deed.) Accustoming the pup to his designated area not only keeps him safe but also avoids his engaging in destructive behaviours when you are not around.

Times of excitement, such as special occasions, family parties, etc., can be fun for the puppy providing that he can view the activities from the security of his designated area. He is not underfoot and he is not being fed all sorts of titbits that will probably cause him stomach distress, yet he still feels a part of the fun.

SCHEDULE
A puppy should be taken to his relief area each time he is released from his designated area, after meals, after a play session and when he first awakens in the morning (at age eight weeks, this can mean 5 a.m.!). The puppy will indicate that he's ready 'to go' by circling or sniffing busily—do not

MEALTIME
Mealtime should be a peaceful time for your puppy. Do not put his food and water bowls in a high-traffic area in the house. For example, give him his own little corner of the kitchen where he can eat undisturbed and where he will not be underfoot. Do not allow small children or other family members to disturb the pup when he is eating.

KEY TO SUCCESS

Success that comes by luck is usually short-lived. Success that comes by well-thought-out proven methods is often more easily achieved and permanent. This is the Success Method. It is designed to give you, the puppy owner, a simple yet proven way to help your puppy develop clean living habits and a feeling of security in his new environment.

misinterpret these signs. For a puppy less than ten weeks of age, a routine of taking him out every hour is necessary. As the puppy grows, he will be able to wait for longer periods of time.

Keep trips to his relief area short. Stay no more than five or six minutes and then return to the house. If he goes during that time, praise him lavishly and take him indoors immediately. If he does not, but he has an accident when you go back indoors, pick him up immediately, say 'No! No!' and return to his relief area. Wait a few minutes, then return to the house again. Never hit a puppy or rub his face in urine or excrement when he has had an accident!

Once indoors, put the puppy in his crate until you have had time to clean up his accident. Then, release him to the family area and watch him more closely

than before. Chances are, his accident was a result of your not picking up his signal or waiting too long before offering him the opportunity to relieve himself. Never hold a grudge against the puppy for accidents.

Let the puppy learn that going outdoors means it is time to relieve himself, not to play. Once trained, he will be able to play indoors and out and still differentiate between the times for play versus the times for relief.

Help him develop regular hours for naps, being alone, playing by himself and just

HOW MANY TIMES A DAY?

AGE	RELIEF TRIPS
To 14 weeks	10
14–22 weeks	8
22–32 weeks	6
Adulthood	4
(dog stops growing)	

These are estimates, of course, but they are a guide to the MINIMUM opportunities a dog should have each day to relieve itself.

resting, all in his crate. Encourage him to entertain himself while you are busy with your activities. Let him learn that having you near is comforting, but it is not your main purpose in life to provide him with undivided attention.

Each time you put your puppy in his own area, use the same command, whatever suits best. Soon he will run to his crate or

Always clean up after your Curly, whether you're in a public place or your own garden.

THE SUCCESS METHOD

6 Steps to Successful Crate Training

1 Tell the puppy 'Crate time!' and place him in the crate with a small treat (a piece of cheese or half of a biscuit). Let him stay in the crate for five minutes while you are in the same room. Then release him and praise lavishly. Never release him when he is fussing. Wait until he is quiet before you let him out.

2 Repeat Step 1 several times a day.

3 The next day, place the puppy in the crate as before. Let him stay there for ten minutes. Do this several times.

4 Continue building time in five-minute increments until the puppy stays in his crate for 30 minutes with you in the room. Always take him to his relief area after prolonged periods in his crate.

5 Now go back to Step 1 and let the puppy stay in his crate for five minutes, this time while you are out of the room.

6 Once again, build crate time in five-minute increments with you out of the room. When the puppy will stay willingly in his crate (he may even fall asleep!) for 30 minutes with you out of the room, he will be ready to stay in it for several hours at a time.

special area when he hears you say those words.

Crate training provides safety for you, the puppy and the home. It also provides the puppy with a feeling of security, and that helps the puppy achieve self-confidence and clean habits. Remember that one of the primary ingredients in house-training your puppy is control. Regardless of your lifestyle, there will always be occasions when you will need to have a place where your dog can stay and be happy and safe. Crate training is the answer for now and in the future.

In conclusion, a few key elements are really all you need for a successful house-training method—consistency, frequency, praise, control and supervision. By following these procedures with a normal, healthy puppy, you and the puppy will soon be past the stage of 'accidents' and ready to move on to a full and rewarding life together.

ROLES OF DISCIPLINE, REWARD AND PUNISHMENT

Discipline, training one to act in accordance with rules, brings order to life. It is as simple as that. Without discipline, particu- larly in a group society, chaos will reign supreme and the group will eventually perish. Humans and canines are social animals and need some form of discipline in order to function effectively. They must procure food, protect their home base and their young and reproduce to keep their species going. If there were no discipline in the lives of social animals, they would eventually die from starva- tion and/or predation by other stronger animals.

In the case of domestic canines, discipline in their lives is needed in order for them to understand how their pack (you and other family members) functions and how they must act in order to survive.

A large humane society in a

THINK BEFORE YOU BARK

Dogs are sensitive to their masters' moods and emotions. Use your voice wisely when communicating with your dog. Never raise your voice at your dog unless you are angry and trying to correct him. 'Barking' at your dog can become as meaningless as 'dogspeak' is to you. Think before you bark!

highly populated area recently surveyed dog owners regarding their satisfaction with their relationships with their dogs. People who had trained their dogs were 75% more satisfied with their pets than those who had never trained their dogs.

Dr Edward Thorndike, a psychologist, established *Thorndike's Theory of Learning*, which states that a behaviour that results in a pleasant event tends to be repeated. A behaviour that results in an unpleasant event tends not to be repeated. It is this theory upon which training methods are based today. For example, if you manipulate a dog to perform a specific behaviour and reward him for doing it, he is likely to do it again because he enjoyed the end result.

Occasionally, punishment, a penalty inflicted for an offence, is necessary. The best type of punishment often comes from an outside source. For example, a child is told not to touch the stove because he may get burned. He disobeys and touches the stove. In doing so, he receives a burn. From that time on, he respects the heat of the stove and avoids contact with it. Therefore, a behaviour that results in an unpleasant event tends not to be repeated.

A good example of a dog learning the hard way is the dog who chases the house cat. He is told many times to leave the cat

FAMILY TIES
If you have other pets in the home and/or interact often with the pets of friends and other family members, your pup will respond to those pets in much the same manner as you do. It is only when you show fear of or resentment toward another animal that he will act fearful or unfriendly.

alone, yet he persists in teasing the cat. Then, one day, the dog begins chasing the cat but the cat turns and swipes a claw across the dog's face, leaving the dog with a painful gash on his nose. The final result is that the dog stops chasing the cat. Again, a behaviour that results in an unpleasant event tends not to be repeated.

PLAN TO PLAY

The puppy should also have regular play and exercise sessions when he is with you or a family member. Exercise for a very young puppy can consist of a short walk around the house or garden. Playing can include fetching games with a large ball or a special raggy. (All puppies teethe and need soft things upon which to chew.) Remember to restrict play periods to indoors within his living area (the family room, for example) until he is completely house-trained.

TRAINING EQUIPMENT

COLLAR AND LEAD

For a Curly Coated Retriever, the collar and lead that you use for training must be one with which you are easily able to work, not too heavy for the dog and perfectly safe.

TREATS

Have a bag of treats on hand; something nutritious and easy to swallow works best. Use a soft treat, a chunk of cheese or a piece of cooked chicken rather than a dry biscuit. By the time the dog has finished chewing a dry treat, he will forget why he is being rewarded in the first place!

Using food rewards will not teach a dog to beg at the table—the only way to teach a dog to beg at the table is to give him food from the table. In training, rewarding the dog with a food treat will help him associate praise and the treats with learning new behaviours that obviously please his owner.

TRAINING BEGINS: ASK THE DOG A QUESTION

In order to teach your dog anything, you must first get his attention. After all, he cannot learn anything if he is looking away from you with his mind on something else.

To get your dog's attention, ask him 'School?' and immediately walk over to him and give him a treat as you tell him 'Good dog.' Wait a minute or two and repeat the routine, this time with a treat in your hand as you approach within a foot of the dog. Do not go directly to him, but stop about a foot short of him and hold out the treat as you ask 'School?' He will see you approaching with a treat in your hand and most likely begin walking toward you. As you meet, give him the treat and praise again.

The third time, ask the question, have a treat in your hand and walk only a short distance toward the dog so that he must walk almost all the way to you. As he reaches you, give him the treat and praise again.

By this time, the dog will probably be getting the idea that if he pays attention to you, especially when you ask that question, it will pay off in treats and enjoyable activities for him. In other words, he learns that 'school' means doing great things with you that are fun and that result in positive attention for him.

Remember that the dog does not understand your verbal language; he only recognises sounds. Your question translates to a series of sounds for him, and those sounds become the signal to go to you and pay attention. The dog learns that if he does this, he will get to interact with you plus receive treats and praise.

THE BASIC COMMANDS

TEACHING SIT
Now that you have the dog's attention, attach his lead and hold it in your left hand, and hold a food treat in your right hand. Place your food hand at the dog's

TRAINING RULES
If you want to be successful in training your dog, you have four rules to obey yourself:
1. Develop an understanding of how a dog thinks.
2. Do not blame the dog for lack of communication.
3. Define your dog's personality and act accordingly.
4. Have patience and be consistent.

The dog should respond naturally to the sit command. If he needs a little encouragement, you can guide him into the position.

relish verbal praise from their owners and feel so proud of themselves whenever they accomplish a behaviour.

You will not use food forever in getting the dog to obey your commands. Food is only used to teach new behaviours and, once the dog knows what you want when you give a specific command, you will wean him off the food treats but still maintain the verbal praise. After all, you will always have your voice with you, and there will be many times when you have no food rewards but expect the dog to obey.

TEACHING DOWN

Teaching the down exercise is easy when you understand how

nose and let him lick the treat but not take it from you. Say 'Sit' and slowly raise your food hand from in front of the dog's nose up over his head so that he is looking at the ceiling. As he bends his head upward, he will have to bend his knees to maintain his balance. As he bends his knees, he will assume a sit position. At that point, release the food treat and praise lavishly with comments such as 'Good dog! Good sit!,' etc. Remember to always praise enthusiastically, because dogs

'NO' MEANS 'NO!'

Dogs do not understand our language. They can be trained to react to a certain sound, at a certain volume. If you say 'No, Oliver' in a very soft pleasant voice, it will not have the same meaning as 'No, Oliver!!' when you shout it as loud as you can. You should never use the dog's name during a reprimand, just the command NO!!

Since dogs don't understand words, comics often use dogs trained with opposite meanings. Thus, when the comic commands his dog to SIT the dog will stand up, and vice versa.

DOUBLE JEOPARDY

A dog in jeopardy never lies down. He stays alert on his feet because instinct tells him that he may have to run away or fight for his survival. Therefore, if a dog feels threatened or anxious, he will not lie down. Consequently, it is important to have the dog calm and relaxed as he learns the down exercise.

the dog perceives the down position, and it is very difficult when you do not. Dogs perceive the down position as a submissive one; therefore, teaching the down exercise by using a forceful method can sometimes make the dog develop such a fear of the down that he either runs away when you say 'Down' or he attempts to snap at the person who tries to force him down.

Have the dog sit close alongside your left leg, facing in the same direction as you are. Hold the lead in your left hand and a food treat in your right. Now place your left hand lightly on the top of the dog's shoulders where they meet above the spinal cord. Do not push down on the dog's shoulders; simply rest your left hand there so you can guide the dog to lie down close to your left leg rather than to swing away from your side when he drops.

Now place the food hand at the dog's nose, say 'Down' very softly (almost a whisper), and slowly lower the food hand to the dog's front feet. When the food hand reaches the floor, begin moving it forward along the floor in front of the dog. Keep talking softly to the dog, saying things like, 'Do you want this treat? You can do this, good dog.' Your reassuring tone of voice will help calm the dog as he tries to follow the food hand in order to get the treat.

When the dog's elbows touch the floor, release the food and praise softly. Try to get the dog to maintain that down position for several seconds before you let him sit up again. The goal here is to get the dog to settle down and not feel threatened in the down position.

TEACHING STAY
It is easy to teach the dog to stay in either a sit or a down position.

Proceed to the down-stay only after the dog has learned the down command. Practise commands in an area that is free from distractions.

CONSISTENCY PAYS OFF

Dogs need consistency in their feeding schedule, exercise and toilet breaks, and in the verbal commands you use. If you use 'Stay' on Monday and 'Stay here, please' on Tuesday, you will confuse your dog. Don't demand perfect behaviour during training classes and then let him have the run of the house the rest of the day. Above all, lavish praise on your pet consistently every time he does something right. The more he feels he is pleasing you, the more willing he will be to learn.

Again, we use food and praise during the teaching process as we help the dog to understand exactly what it is that we are expecting him to do.

To teach the sit/stay, start with the dog sitting on your left side as before and hold the lead in your left hand. Have a food treat in your right hand and place your food hand at the dog's nose. Say 'Stay' and step out on your right foot to stand directly in front of the dog, toe to toe, as he licks and nibbles the treat. Be sure to keep his head facing upward to maintain the sit position. Count to five and then swing around to stand next to the dog again with him on your left. As soon as you get back to the original position, release the food and praise lavishly.

To teach the down/stay, do the down as previously described. As soon as the dog lies down, say 'Stay' and step out on your right

SAFETY FIRST

While it may seem that the most important things to your dog are eating, sleeping and chewing the upholstery on your furniture, his first concern is actually safety. The domesticated dogs we keep as companions have the same pack instinct as their ancestors who ran free thousands of years ago. Because of this pack instinct, your dog wants to know that he and his pack are not in danger of being harmed, and that his pack has a strong, capable leader. You must establish yourself as the leader early on in your relationship. That way your dog will trust that you will take care of him and the pack, and he will accept your commands without question.

foot just as you did in the sit/stay. Count to five and then return to stand beside the dog with him on your left side. Release the treat and praise as always.

Within a week or ten days, you can begin to add a bit of distance between you and your dog when you leave him. When you do, use your left hand open with the palm facing the dog as a stay signal, much the same as the hand signal a constable uses to stop traffic at an intersection. Hold the food treat in your right hand as before, but this time the food will not be touching the dog's nose. He will watch the food hand and quickly learn that he is going to get that treat as soon as you return to his side.

When you can stand 1 metre away from your dog for 30 seconds, you can then begin building time and distance in both stays. Eventually, the dog can be expected to remain in the stay position for prolonged periods of time until you return to him or call him to you. Always praise lavishly when he stays.

TEACHING COME

If you make teaching 'come' an exciting experience, you should never have a 'student' that does not love the game or that fails to come when called. The secret, it seems, is never to teach the word 'come.'

At times when an owner most

FEAR AGGRESSION

Pups who are subjected to physical abuse during training commonly end up with behavioural problems as adults. One common result of abuse is fear aggression, in which a dog will lash out, bare his teeth, snarl and finally bite someone by whom he feels threatened. For example, your daughter may be playing with the dog one afternoon. As they play hide-and-seek, she backs the dog into a corner and, as she attempts to tease him playfully, he bites her hand. Examine the cause of this behaviour. Did your daughter ever hit the dog? Did someone who resembles your daughter hit or scream at the dog?

Fortunately, fear aggression is relatively easy to correct. Have your daughter engage in only positive activities with the dog, such as feeding, petting and walking. She should not give any corrections or negative feedback. If the dog still growls or cowers away from her, allow someone else to accompany them. After approximately one week, the dog should feel that he can rely on her for many positive things, and he will also be prevented from reacting fearfully towards anyone who might resemble her.

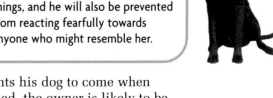

wants his dog to come when called, the owner is likely to be upset or anxious and he allows these feelings to come through in

'WHERE ARE YOU?'

When calling the dog, do not say 'Come.' Say things like, 'Rover, where are you? See if you can find me! I have a biscuit for you!' Keep up a constant line of chatter with coaxing sounds and frequent questions such as, 'Where are you?' The dog will learn to follow the sound of your voice to locate you and receive his reward.

Everyone takes turns calling the dog, and each person should celebrate the dog's finding him with a treat and lots of happy praise. When a person calls the dog, he is actually inviting the dog to find him and to get a treat as a reward for 'winning.'

A few turns of the 'Where are you?' game and the dog will understand that everyone is playing the game and that each person has a big celebration awaiting the dog's success at locating him or her. Once the dog learns to love the game, simply calling out 'Where are you?' will have him running from wherever he is when he hears that all-important question.

The come command is recognised as one of the most important things to teach a dog, but there are trainers who work with thousands of dogs and never teach the actual word 'Come.' Yet these dogs will race to respond to a person who uses the dog's name

the tone of his voice when he calls his dog. Hearing that desperation in his owner's voice, the dog fears the results of going to him and therefore either disobeys outright or runs in the opposite direction. The secret, therefore, is to teach the dog a game and, when you want him to come to you, simply play the game. It is practically a no-fail solution!

To begin, have several members of your family take a few food treats and each go into a different room in the house.

'COME' ... BACK

Never call your dog to come to you for a correction or scold him when he reaches you. That is the quickest way to turn a 'Come' command into 'Go away fast!' Dogs think only in the present tense, and your dog will connect the scolding with coming to you, not with the misbehaviour of a few moments earlier.

your left hand as the dog sits beside your left leg. Move the loop end of the lead to your right hand, but keep your left hand short on the lead so that it keeps the dog in close next to you.

Say 'Heel' and step forward on your left foot. Keep the dog close to you and take three steps. Stop and have the dog sit next to you in what we now call the 'heel

followed by 'Where are you?' For example, a woman has a 12-year-old companion dog who went blind, but who never fails to locate her owner when asked, 'Where are you?'

Children, in particular, love to play this game with their dogs. Children can hide in smaller places like a shower or bath, behind a bed or under a table. The dog needs to work a little bit harder to find these hiding places, but, when he does, he loves to celebrate with a treat and a tussle with a favourite youngster.

TEACHING HEEL

Heeling means that the dog walks beside the owner without pulling. It takes time and patience on the owner's part to succeed at teaching the dog that he (the owner) will not proceed unless the dog is walking calmly beside him. Neither pulling out ahead on the lead nor lagging behind is acceptable.

Begin by holding the lead in

HEELING WELL

Teach your dog to heel in an enclosed area. Once you think the dog will obey reliably and you want to attempt advanced obedience exercises such as off-lead heeling, test him in a fenced-in area so he cannot run away.

position.' Praise verbally, but do not touch the dog. Hesitate a moment and begin again with 'Heel,' taking three steps and stopping, at which point the dog is told to sit again.

Your goal here is to have the dog walk those three steps without pulling on the lead. Once he will walk calmly beside you for three steps without pulling, increase the number of steps you take to five. When he will walk politely beside

Heel training is necessary, since on-lead walks should be a part of your Curly's daily exercise.

you while you take five steps, you can increase the length of your walk to ten steps. Keep increasing the length of your stroll until the dog will walk quietly beside you without pulling as long as you want him to heel. When you stop heeling, indicate to the dog that the exercise is over by verbally praising as you pet him and say 'OK, good dog.' The 'OK' is used as a release word, meaning that the exercise is finished and the dog is free to relax.

If you are dealing with a dog who insists on pulling you around, simply 'put on your brakes' and stand your ground until the dog realises that the two of you are not going anywhere until he is beside you and moving at your pace, not his. It may take some time just standing there to convince the dog that you are the leader and that you will be the one to decide on the direction and speed of your travel.

Each time the dog looks up at you or slows down to give a slack lead between the two of you, quietly praise him and say, 'Good heel. Good dog.' Eventually, the dog will begin to respond and within a few days he will be walking politely beside you without pulling on the lead. At first, the training sessions should be kept short and very positive; soon the dog will be able to walk nicely with you for increasingly longer distances. Remember also to give the dog free time and the opportunity to run and play when you have finished heel practice.

WEANING OFF FOOD IN TRAINING

Food is used in training new behaviours. Once the dog understands what behaviour goes with a specific command, it is time to start weaning him off the food treats. At first, give a treat after each exercise. Then, start to give a treat only after every other exercise. Mix up the times when you offer a food reward and the times when you only offer praise so that the dog will never know when he is going to receive both food and praise and when he is going to receive only praise. This is called a variable ratio reward system. It proves successful because there is always the chance that the owner will produce a treat, so the dog never stops trying for that reward. No matter what, ALWAYS give verbal praise.

OBEDIENCE CLASSES

It is a good idea to enrol in an obedience class if one is available in your area. If yours is a show dog, ringcraft classes would be more appropriate. Many areas have dog clubs that offer basic obedience training as well as preparatory classes for obedience competition. There are also local dog trainers who

HOW TO WEAN THE 'TREAT HOG'

If you have trained your dog by rewarding him with a treat each time he performs a command, he may soon decide that without the treat, he won't sit, stay or come. The best way to fix this problem is to start asking your dog to do certain commands twice before being rewarded. Slowly increase the number of commands given and then vary the number: three sits and a treat one day, five sits for a biscuit the next day, etc. Your dog will soon realise that there is no set number of sits before he gets his reward, and he'll likely do it the first time you ask in the hope of being rewarded sooner rather than later.

offer similar classes.

At obedience shows, dogs can earn titles at various levels of competition. The beginning levels of obedience competition include basic behaviours such as sit, down, heel, etc. The more advanced levels of competition include jumping, retrieving, scent discrimination and signal work. The advanced levels require a dog and owner to put a lot of time and effort into their training. The titles that can be earned at these levels of competition are very prestigious. Although the Curly is not as precise at obedience as the Golden or the Labrador, the breed has become more popular in obedience competition, and is capable of achieving a noteworthy degree of success in the obedience ring. Curlies learn quickly if proper training methods are applied. Because they have such an active mentality with a short attention span, they bore easily, which is a challenge for the average pet owner/trainer. However, in the United States, several Curlies have achieved obedience championships in both AKC and United Kennel Club competition.

OTHER ACTIVITIES FOR LIFE

Whether a dog is trained in the structured environment of a class or alone with his owner at home, there are many activities that can bring fun and rewards to both

OBEDIENCE SCHOOL

Taking your dog to an obedience school may be the best investment in time and money you can ever make. You will enjoy the benefits for the lifetime of your dog and you will have the opportunity to meet people who have similar expectations for companion dogs.

owner and dog once they have mastered basic control.

Teaching the dog to help out around the home, in the garden or on the farm provides great satisfaction to both dog and owner. In addition, the dog's help makes life a little easier for his owner and raises his stature as a valued companion to his family. It helps give the dog a purpose by occupying his mind and providing an outlet for his energy.

Backpacking is an exciting and healthy activity that the dog can be taught without assistance from more than his owner. The exercise of walking and climbing is good for man and dog alike, and the bond that they develop together is priceless. The rule for backpacking with any dog is never to expect the dog to carry more than one-sixth of his body weight.

If you are interested in participating in organised competition with your Curly Coated Retriever, there are activities other than obedience in which you and your dog can become involved. Agility is a popular sport in which dogs run through a timed obstacle course that includes various jumps, tunnels and other exercises to test the dog's speed and coordination. The owners run beside their dogs to give commands and to guide them through the course. Although competitive, the focus is on fun— it's fun to do, fun to watch and great exercise.

Field and gundog trials, along with working trials, are popular types of competition for Curlies, as these areas of the dog sport enable the breed to develop and utilise its instinctive abilities. These trials require higher levels of training, but are well suited to the breed and are a welcome outlet for the Curly's talent and energy.

Flyball is a team event in which the dogs run a series of jumps while carrying a ball over a specified course of hurdles. Several dogs comprise a flyball team, and the event is timed, making speed of the essence. The Curly is a natural for the sport, and more Curly owners are entering flyball competitions with their dogs.

Most trainers use a dummy to begin retriever training. This will be your Curly's favourite exercise because it involves the breed's most natural ability. Throw the dummy (inset) only when you have the dog's attention.

Recognise the signs of good health in your Curly Coated Retriever.

Your Curly must always be under your supervision. Report any abnormalities in his behaviour to the vet immediately.

Dogs suffer from many of the same physical illnesses as people. They might even share many of the same psychological problems. Since people usually know more about human diseases than canine maladies, many of the terms used in this chapter will be familiar but not necessarily those used by veterinary surgeons. We will use the term *x-ray*, instead of the more acceptable term *radiograph*. We will also use the familiar term *symptoms* even though dogs don't have symptoms, which are verbal descriptions of the patient's feelings; dogs have *clinical signs*. Since dogs can't speak, we have to look for clinical signs...but we still use the term *symptoms* in this book.

As a general rule, medicine is *practised*. That term is not arbitrary. Medicine is a constantly changing art as we learn more and more about genetics, electronic aids (like CAT scans) and daily laboratory advances. There are many dog maladies, like canine hip dysplasia, which are not universally treated in the same manner. Some veterinary surgeons opt for surgery more often than others do.

SELECTING A VETERINARY SURGEON

Your selection of a veterinary surgeon should not be based upon personality (as most are) but upon their convenience to your home. You want a vet who is close

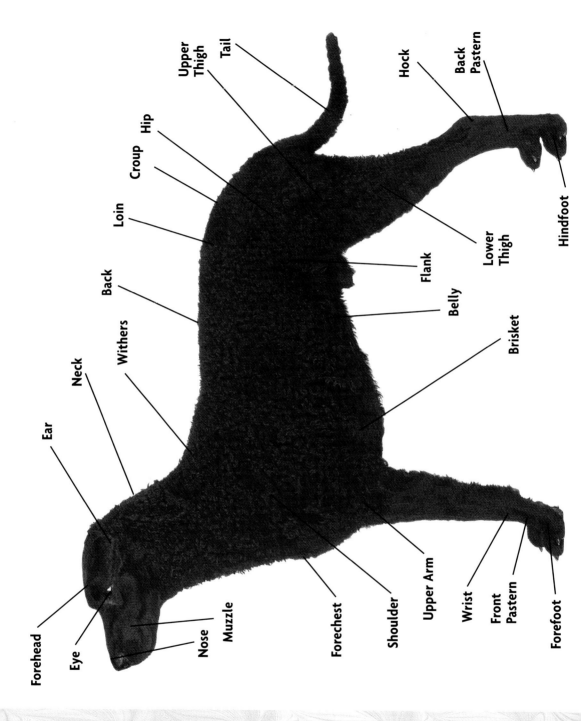

PHYSICAL STRUCTURE OF THE CURLY COATED RETRIEVER

because you might have emergencies or need to make multiple visits for treatments. You want a vet who has services that you might require such as tattooing and grooming, as well as sophisticated pet supplies and a good reputation for ability and responsiveness. There is nothing more frustrating than having to wait a day or more to get a response from your veterinary surgeon.

All veterinary surgeons are licensed and their diplomas and/or certificates should be displayed in their waiting rooms. There are, however, many veterinary specialities that usually require further studies and internships. There are specialists in heart problems (veterinary cardiologists), skin problems (veterinary dermatologists), teeth and gum problems (veterinary dentists), eye problems (veterinary ophthalmologists) and x-rays (veterinary radiologists), as well as vets who have specialities in bones, muscles or other organs. Most veterinary surgeons do routine surgery such as neutering, stitching up wounds and docking tails for those breeds in which such is required for show purposes.

When the problem affecting your dog is serious, it is not unusual or impudent to get another medical opinion, although in Britain you are obliged to advise the vets concerned about

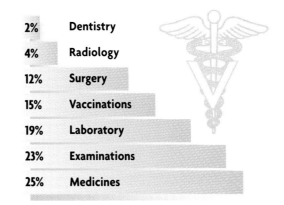

Breakdown of Veterinary Income by Category

2%	Dentistry
4%	Radiology
12%	Surgery
15%	Vaccinations
19%	Laboratory
23%	Examinations
25%	Medicines

this. You might also want to compare costs among several veterinary surgeons. Sophisticated health care and veterinary services can be very costly. It is not infrequent that important decisions are based upon financial considerations.

PREVENTATIVE MEDICINE
It is much easier, less costly and more effective to practise preventative medicine than to fight bouts of illness and disease. Properly bred puppies come from parents who were selected based upon their genetic disease profiles. Their mothers should have been vaccinated, free of all internal and external parasites and properly nourished. The dam can pass on disease resistance to her puppies, which can last for eight to ten weeks, but she can also pass on

A typical American vet's income, categorised according to services performed. This survey dealt with small-animal (pets) practices.

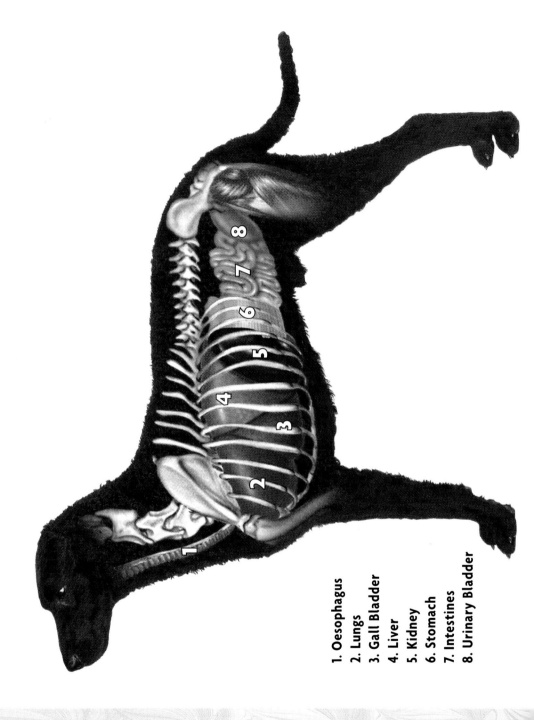

1. Oesophagus
2. Lungs
3. Gall Bladder
4. Liver
5. Kidney
6. Stomach
7. Intestines
8. Urinary Bladder

INTERNAL ORGANS OF THE CURLY COATED RETRIEVER

parasites and many infections. For these reasons, a visit to the veterinary surgeon who cared for the dam is recommended.

VACCINATION SCHEDULING

Most vaccinations are given by injection and should only be done by a veterinary surgeon. Both he and you should keep records of the date of the injection, the identification of the vaccine and the amount given. Some vets give a first vaccination at eight weeks, but most dog breeders prefer the course not to commence until about ten weeks to avoid negating any antibodies passed on by the dam. The vaccination scheduling is usually based on a 15-day cycle. You must take your vet's advice regarding when to vaccinate, as this may differ according to the vaccine used. Most vaccinations immunize your puppy against viruses.

The usual vaccines contain immunizing doses of several different viruses such as distemper, parvovirus, parainfluenza and hepatitis, although some veterinary surgeons recommend separate vaccines for each disease. There are other vaccines available when the puppy is at risk. You should rely

HEALTH AND VACCINATION SCHEDULE

AGE IN WEEKS:	6TH	8TH	10TH	12TH	14TH	16TH	20-24TH	1 YR
Worm Control	✔	✔	✔	✔	✔	✔	✔	
Neutering								✔
Heartworm		✔		✔		✔	✔	
Parvovirus	✔		✔		✔		✔	✔
Distemper		✔		✔		✔		✔
Hepatitis		✔		✔		✔		✔
Leptospirosis								✔
Parainfluenza	✔		✔		✔			✔
Dental Examination		✔					✔	✔
Complete Physical		✔					✔	✔
Coronavirus				✔			✔	✔
Kennel Cough	✔							
Hip Dysplasia								✔
Rabies							✔	

Vaccinations are not instantly effective. It takes about two weeks for the dog's immune system to develop antibodies. Most vaccinations require annual booster shots. Your veterinary surgeon should guide you in this regard.

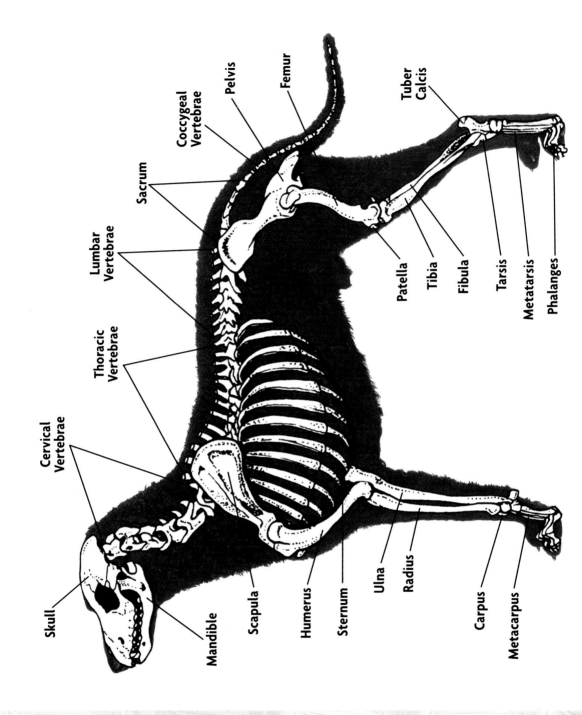

Coccygeal
Vertebrae

Pelvis

Femur

Tuber
Calcis

Sacrum

Lumbar
Vertebrae

Patella

Tibia

Fibula

Tarsis

Metatarsis

Phalanges

Thoracic
Vertebrae

Cervical
Vertebrae

Skull

Mandible

Scapula

Humerus

Sternum

Ulna

Radius

Carpus

Metacarpus

SKELETAL STRUCTURE OF THE CURLY COATED RETRIEVER

upon professional advice. This is especially true for the booster-shot programme. Most vaccination programmes require a booster when the puppy is a year old and once a year thereafter. In some cases, circumstances may require more or less frequent immunizations. Kennel cough, more formally known as tracheobronchitis, is treated with a vaccine that is sprayed into the dog's nostrils. Kennel cough is usually included in routine vaccination, but this is often not so effective as for other major diseases.

WEANING TO FIVE MONTHS OLD

Puppies should be weaned by the time they are about two months old. A puppy that remains for at least eight weeks with its mother and littermates usually adapts better to other dogs and people later in life. Some new owners have their puppies examined by veterinary surgeons immediately, which is a good idea. Vaccination programmes usually begin when the puppy is very young.

The puppy will have its teeth examined, and have its skeletal conformation and general health

DISEASE REFERENCE CHART

	What is it?	What causes it?	Symptoms
Leptospirosis	Severe disease that affects the internal organs; can be spread to people.	A bacterium, which is often carried by rodents, that enters through mucous membranes and spreads quickly throughout the body.	Range from fever, vomiting and loss of appetite in less severe cases to shock, irreversible kidney damage and possibly death in most severe cases.
Rabies	Potentially deadly virus that infects warm-blooded mammals. Not seen in United Kingdom.	Bite from a carrier of the virus, mainly wild animals.	1st stage: dog exhibits change in behaviour, fear. 2nd stage: dog's behaviour becomes more aggressive. 3rd stage: loss of coordination, trouble with bodily functions.
Parvovirus	Highly contagious virus, potentially deadly.	Ingestion of the virus, which is usually spread through the faeces of infected dogs.	Most common: severe diarrhoea. Also vomiting, fatigue, lack of appetite.
Kennel cough	Contagious respiratory infection.	Combination of types of bacteria and virus. Most common: *Bordetella bronchiseptica* bacteria and parainfluenza virus.	Chronic cough.
Distemper	Disease primarily affecting respiratory and nervous system.	Virus that is related to the human measles virus.	Mild symptoms such as fever, lack of appetite and mucous secretion progress to evidence of brain damage, 'hard pad.'
Hepatitis	Virus primarily affecting the liver.	Canine adenovirus type I (CAV-1). Enters system when dog breathes in particles.	Lesser symptoms include listlessness, diarrhoea, vomiting. More severe symptoms include 'blue-eye' (clumps of virus in eye).
Coronavirus	Virus resulting in digestive problems.	Virus is spread through infected dog's faeces.	Stomach upset evidenced by lack of appetite, vomiting, diarrhoea.

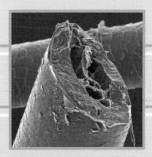

Normal hairs of a dog enlarged 200 times original size. The cuticle (outer covering) is clean and healthy. Unlike human hair that grows from the base, a dog's hair also grows from the end. Damaged hairs and split ends, illustrated above.

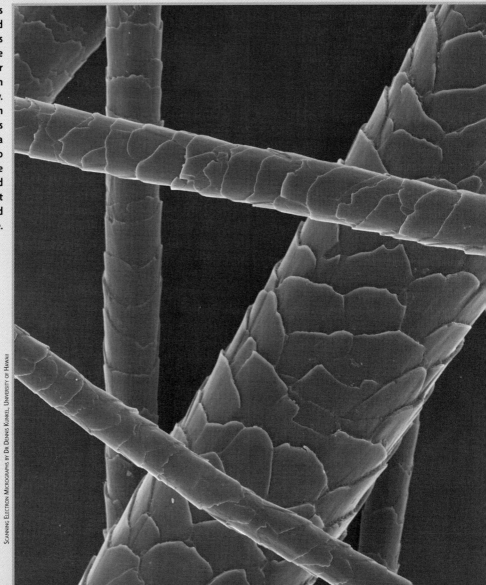

SCANNING ELECTRON MICROGRAPHS BY DR. DENNIS KUNKEL, UNIVERSITY OF HAWAII

checked prior to certification by the veterinary surgeon. Puppies in certain breeds may have problems with their kneecaps, cataracts and other eye problems, heart murmurs or undescended testicles. They may also have personality problems, and your veterinary surgeon might have training in temperament evaluation.

FIVE TO TWELVE MONTHS OF AGE
Unless you intend to breed or show your dog, neutering the puppy at six months of age is recommended. Discuss this with your veterinary surgeon. Neutering has proven to be extremely beneficial to both male and female puppies. Besides eliminating the possibility of pregnancy, it inhibits (but does not prevent) breast cancer in bitches and prostate cancer in male dogs. Under no circumstances should a bitch be spayed prior to her first season.

Your veterinary surgeon should provide your puppy with a thorough dental evaluation at six months of age, ascertaining whether all the permanent teeth have erupted properly. A home dental care regimen should be initiated at six months, including brushing weekly and providing good dental devices (such as nylon bones). Regular dental care promotes healthy teeth, fresh breath and a longer life.

ONE TO SEVEN YEARS
Once a year, your grown dog should visit the vet for an examination and vaccination boosters, if needed. Some vets recommend blood tests, a thyroid level check and a dental evaluation to accompany these annual visits. A thorough clinical evaluation by the vet can provide critical background information for your dog. Blood tests are often performed at one year of age, and dental examinations around the third or fourth birthday. In the long run, quality preventative care for your pet can save money, teeth and lives.

SKIN PROBLEMS IN CURLY COATED RETRIEVERS
Veterinary surgeons are consulted by dog owners for skin problems more than for any other group of

CARETAKER OF TEETH
You are your dog's caretaker and his dentist. Vets warn that plaque and tartar buildup on the teeth will damage the gums and allow bacteria to enter the dog's bloodstream, causing serious damage to the animal's vital organs. Studies show that over 50 percent of dogs have some form of gum disease before age three. Daily or weekly tooth cleaning (with a brush or soft gauze pad wipes) can add to your dog's life.

diseases or maladies. Dogs' skin is almost as sensitive as human skin, and both suffer from almost the same ailments (though the occurrence of acne in dogs is rare!). For this reason, veterinary dermatology has developed into a speciality practised by many veterinary surgeons.

Since many skin problems have visual symptoms that are almost identical, it requires the skill of an experienced veterinary dermatologist to identify and cure many of the more severe skin disorders. Pet shops sell many treatments for skin problems, but most of the treatments are directed at the symptoms and not the underlying problem(s). If your dog is suffering from a skin disorder, you should seek professional assistance as quickly as possible. As with all diseases, the earlier a problem is identified and treated, the more successful is the cure.

HEREDITARY SKIN DISORDERS

Veterinary dermatologists are currently researching a number of skin disorders that are believed to have an hereditary basis. These inherited diseases are transmitted by both parents, who appear (phenotypically) normal but have a recessive gene for the disease, meaning that they carry, but are not affected by, the disease. These diseases pose serious problems to breeders because in some

> **KNOW WHEN TO POSTPONE A VACCINATION**
>
> While the visit to the vet is costly, it is never advisable to update a vaccination when visiting with a sick or pregnant dog. Vaccinations should be avoided for all elderly dogs. If your dog is showing the signs of any illness or any medical condition, no matter how serious or mild, including skin irritations, do not vaccinate. Likewise, a lame dog should never be vaccinated; any dog undergoing surgery or on any immunosuppressant drugs should not be vaccinated until fully recovered.

instances there are no methods of identifying carriers. Often the secondary diseases associated with these skin conditions are even more debilitating than the skin disorders themselves, including cancers and respiratory problems; others can be lethal.

Among the hereditary skin disorders, for which the mode of inheritance is known, are acrodermatitis, cutaneous asthenia (Ehlers-Danlos syndrome), sebaceous adenitis, cyclic hematopoiesis, dermatomyositis, IgA deficiency, colour dilution alopecia and nodular dermatofibrosis. Some of these disorders are limited to one or two breeds, while others affect a large number of breeds. All inherited diseases must be diagnosed and treated by a veterinary specialist.

PARASITE BITES

Many of us are allergic to insect bites. The bites itch, erupt and may even become infected. Dogs have the same reaction to fleas, ticks and/or mites. When an insect lands on you, you have the chance to whisk it away with your hand. Unfortunately, when your dog is bitten by a flea, tick or mite, he can only scratch it away or bite it. By the time the dog has been bitten, the parasite has done some of its damage. It may also have laid eggs, which will cause further problems in the near future. The itching from parasite bites is probably due to the saliva injected into the site when the parasite sucks the dog's blood.

AUTO-IMMUNE SKIN CONDITIONS

An auto-immune skin condition is commonly referred to as a condition in which a person (or dog) is 'allergic' to him- or herself, while an allergy is usually an inflammatory reaction to an outside stimulus. Auto-immune diseases cause serious damage to the tissues that are involved.

The best known auto-immune disease is lupus, which affects people as well as dogs. The symptoms are variable and may affect the kidneys, bones, blood chemistry and skin. It can be fatal to both dogs and humans, though it is not thought to be transmissible. It is usually successfully treated with cortisone, prednisone or a similar corticosteroid, but extensive use of these drugs can have harmful side effects.

ACRAL LICK GRANULOMA

Many large dogs have a very poorly understood syndrome called acral lick granuloma. The manifestation of the problem is the dog's tireless attack at a specific area of the body, almost

PET ADVANTAGES

If you do not intend to show or breed your new puppy, your veterinary surgeon will probably recommend that you spay your female or neuter your male. Some people believe neutering leads to weight gain, but if you feed and exercise your dog properly, this is easily avoided. Spaying or neutering can actually have many positive outcomes, such as:

- training becomes easier, as the dog focuses less on the urge to mate and more on you!
- females are protected from unplanned pregnancy as well as ovarian and uterine cancers.
- males are guarded from testicular tumours and have a reduced risk of developing prostate cancer.

Talk to your vet regarding the right age to spay/neuter and other aspects of the procedure.

always the legs or paws. The dog licks so intensively that he removes the hair and skin, leaving an ugly, large wound. Tiny protuberances, which are outgrowths of new capillaries, bead on the surface of the wound. Owners who notice their dogs' biting and chewing at their extremities should have the vet determine the cause. If lick granuloma is identified, although there is no absolute cure, corticosteroids are the most common treatment.

AIRBORNE ALLERGIES

An interesting allergy is pollen allergy. Humans have hay fever, rose fever and other fevers from which they suffer during the pollinating season. Many dogs suffer the same allergies. When the pollen count is high, your dog might suffer, but don't expect him to sneeze and have a runny nose like a human would. Dogs react to pollen allergies the same way they react to fleas—they scratch and bite themselves.

Dogs, like humans, can be tested for allergens. Discuss the testing with your veterinary dermatologist.

FOOD PROBLEMS

FOOD ALLERGIES

Dogs are allergic to many foods that are best-sellers and highly recommended by breeders and veterinary surgeons. Changing the brand of food that you buy may not eliminate the problem if the element to which the dog is allergic is contained in the new brand.

Recognising a food allergy is difficult. Humans vomit or have rashes when they eat a food to which they are allergic. Dogs neither vomit nor (usually) develop rashes. They react in the same manner as they would to an airborne or flea allergy: they itch, scratch and bite, thus making the diagnosis extremely difficult. While pollen allergies and parasite bites are usually seasonal, food allergies are year-round problems.

VITAL SIGNS

A dog's normal temperature is 38.6° Celsius (101.5° Fahrenheit). A range of between 37.8-39.2° Celsius (100.0 and 102.5° Fahrenheit) should be considered normal, as each dog's body sets its own temperature. It will be helpful if you take your dog's temperature when you know he is healthy and record it. Then, when you suspect that he is not feeling well, you will have a normal figure to compare the abnormal temperature against.

The normal pulse rate for a dog is between 100 and 125 beats per minute.

FOOD INTOLERANCE

Food intolerance is the inability of the dog to completely digest certain foods. Puppies that may have done very well on their mother's milk may not do well on cow's milk. The results of food intolerance may be evident in loose bowels, passing gas and stomach pains. These are the only obvious symptoms of food intolerance, which makes diagnosis difficult.

TREATING FOOD PROBLEMS

It is possible to handle food allergies and food intolerance yourself. Start by putting your dog on a diet that he has never had. Obviously, if the dog has never eaten this new food, he can't have been allergic or intolerant of it. Start with a single ingredient that is not in the dog's diet at the present time. Ingredients like chopped beef or fish are common in dogs' diets, so try something more exotic like rabbit, pheasant or even just vegetables. Keep the dog on this diet (with no additives) for a month. If the symptoms of food allergy or intolerance disappear, it is quite likely that your dog has a food allergy.

Don't think that the single ingredient cured the problem. You still must find a suitable diet and ascertain which ingredient in the old diet was

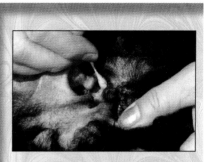

MANY KINDS OF EARS
Not every dog's ears are the same. Ears that are open to the air are healthier than ears with poor air circulation. Sometimes a dog can have two differently shaped ears. You should not probe inside your dog's ears as shown above. Instead, only clean that which is accessible with a soft cotton wipe.

objectionable. This is most easily done by adding ingredients to the new diet one at a time. Let the dog stay on the modified diet for a month before you add another ingredient. Eventually, you will determine the ingredient that caused the adverse reaction.

An alternative method is to carefully study the ingredients in the diet to which your dog is allergic or intolerant. Identify the main ingredient in this diet and eliminate the main ingredient by buying a different food that does not have that ingredient. Keep experimenting until the symptoms disappear after one month on the new diet.

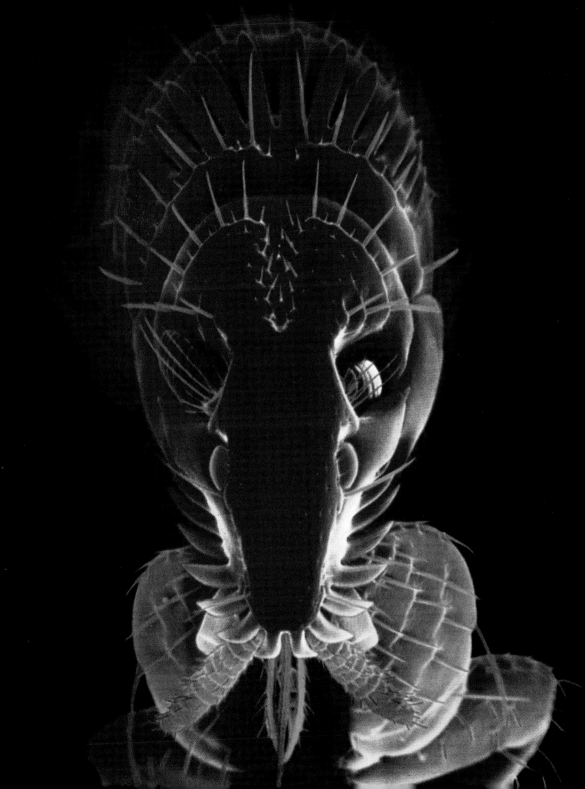

EXTERNAL PARASITES

FLEAS

Of all the problems to which dogs are prone, none is more well known and frustrating than fleas. Flea infestation is relatively simple to cure but difficult to prevent. Parasites that are harboured inside the body are a bit more difficult to eradicate but they are easier to control.

To control flea infestation, you have to understand the flea's life cycle. Fleas are often thought of as a summertime problem, but centrally heated homes have changed the patterns and fleas can be found at any time of the year. The most effective method of flea control is a two-stage approach: one stage to kill the adult fleas, and the other to control the development of pre-adult fleas. Unfortunately, no single active ingredient is effective against all stages of the life cycle.

Magnified head of a dog flea, *Ctenocephalides canis.*

LIFE CYCLE STAGES

During its life, a flea will pass through four life stages: egg, larva, pupa and adult. The adult stage is the most visible and irritating stage of the flea life cycle, and this is

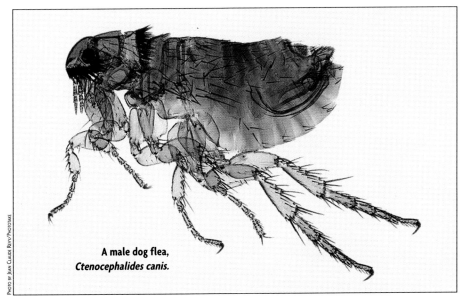

A male dog flea, *Ctenocephalides canis.*

Opposite page: A scanning electron micrograph of a dog or cat flea, *Ctenocephalides,* magnified more than 100x. This image has been colorized for effect.

S. E. M. BY DR DENNIS KUNKEL, UNIVERSITY OF HAWAII

PHOTO BY JEAN CLAUDE REVY/PHOTOTAKE

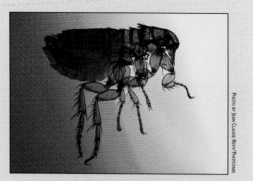

Photo by Jean Claude Revy/Phototake

A LOOK AT FLEAS

Fleas have been around for millions of years and have adapted to changing host animals. They are able to go through a complete life cycle in less than one month or they can extend their lives to almost two years by remaining as pupae or cocoons. They do not need blood or any other food for up to 20 months.

They have been measured as being able to jump 300,000 times and can jump 150 times their length in any direction, including straight up. Those are just a few of the reasons why they are so successful in infesting a dog!

FLEA KILLERS

Flea-killers are poisonous. You should not spray these toxic chemicals on areas of a dog's body that he licks, on his genitals or on his face. Flea killers taken internally are a better answer, but check with your vet in case internal therapy is not advised for your dog.

why the majority of flea-control products concentrate on this stage. The fact is that adult fleas account for only 1% of the total flea population, and the other 99% exist in pre-adult stages, i.e. eggs, larvae and pupae. The pre-adult stages are barely visible to the naked eye.

THE LIFE CYCLE OF THE FLEA

Eggs are laid on the dog, usually in quantities of about 20 or 30, several times a day. The female adult flea must have a blood meal before each egg-laying session. When first laid, the eggs will cling to the dog's hair, as the eggs are still moist.

The Life Cycle of the Flea

Photos courtesy of Fleabusters® Rx for Fleas.

Eggs   **Larvae**   **Pupa**   **Adult**

However, they will quickly dry out and fall from the dog, especially if the dog moves around or scratches. Many eggs will fall off in the dog's favourite area or an area in which he spends a lot of time, such as his bed.

Once the eggs fall from the dog onto the carpet or furniture, they will hatch into larvae. This takes from one to ten days. Larvae are not particularly mobile and will usually travel only a few inches from where they hatch. However, they do have a tendency to move away from light and heavy traffic—under furniture and behind doors are common places to find high quantities of flea larvae.

The flea larvae feed on dead organic matter, including adult flea faeces, until they are ready to change into adult fleas. Fleas will usually remain as larvae for around seven days. After this period, the larvae will pupate into protective pupae. While inside the pupae, the larvae will undergo metamorphosis and change into adult fleas. This can take as little time as a few days, but the adult fleas can remain inside the pupae waiting to hatch for up to two years. The pupae are signalled to hatch by certain stimuli, such as physical pressure—the pupae's being stepped on, heat from an animal lying on the pupae or increased carbon dioxide levels and vibrations—indicating that a suitable host is available.

Once hatched, the adult flea must feed within a few days. Once the adult flea finds a host, it will not leave voluntarily. It only becomes dislodged by grooming or the host animal's scratching. The adult flea will remain on the host for the duration of its life unless forcibly removed.

INSECT GROWTH REGULATOR (IGR)

Two types of products should be used when treating fleas—a product to treat the pet and a product to treat the home. Adult fleas represent less than 1% of the flea population. The pre-adult fleas (eggs, larvae and pupae) represent more than 99% of the flea population and are found in the environment; it is in the case of pre-adult fleas that products containing an Insect Growth Regulator (IGR) should be used in the home.

IGRs are a new class of compounds used to prevent the development of insects. They do not kill the insect outright, but instead use the insect's biology against it to stop it from completing its growth. Products that contain methoprene are the world's first and leading IGRs. Used to control fleas and other insects, this type of IGR will stop flea larvae from developing and protect the house for up to seven months.

A scanning electron micrograph (S. E. M.) of a dog flea, *Ctenocephalides canis.*

S. E. M. BY DR DENNIS KUNKEL, UNIVERSITY OF HAWAII

actually mimic the fleas' own hormones and stop the eggs and larvae from developing into adult fleas. There are currently no treatments available to attack the pupa stage of the life cycle, so the adult insecticide is used to kill the newly hatched adult fleas before they find a host. Most IGRs are active for many months, while adult insecticides are only active for a few days.

TREATING THE ENVIRONMENT AND THE DOG

Treating fleas should be a two-pronged attack. First, the environment needs to be treated; this includes carpets and furniture, especially the dog's bedding and areas underneath furniture. The environment should be treated with a household spray containing an Insect Growth Regulator (IGR) and an insecticide to kill the adult fleas. Most IGRs are effective against eggs and larvae; they

Dwight R Kuhn's magnificent action photo, showing a flea jumping from a dog's back.

PHOTO BY DWIGHT R KUHN

EN GARDE: CATCHING FLEAS OFF GUARD!

Consider the following ways to arm yourself against fleas:
• Add a small amount of pennyroyal or eucalyptus oil to your dog's bath. These natural remedies repel fleas.
• Supplement your dog's food with fresh garlic (minced or grated) and a hearty amount of brewer's yeast, both of which ward off fleas.
• Use a flea comb on your dog daily. Submerge fleas in a cup of bleach to kill them quickly.
• Confine the dog to only a few rooms to limit the spread of fleas in the home.
• Vacuum daily...and get all of the crevices! Dispose of the bag every few days until the problem is under control.
• Wash your dog's bedding daily. Cover cushions where your dog sleeps with towels, and wash the towels often.

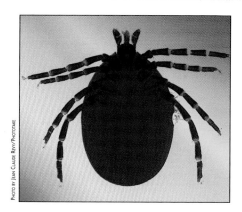

PHOTO BY JEAN CLAUDE REVY/PHOTOTAKE

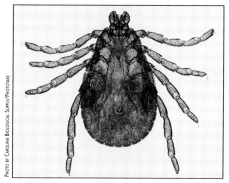

PHOTO BY CAROLINA BIOLOGICAL SUPPLY/PHOTOTAKE

When treating with a household spray, it is a good idea to vacuum before applying the product. This stimulates as many pupae as possible to hatch into adult fleas. The vacuum cleaner

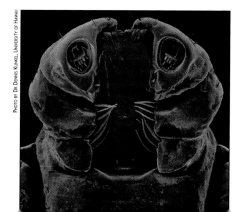

PHOTO BY DR DENNIS KUNKEL, UNIVERSITY OF HAWAII

should also be treated with an insecticide to prevent the eggs and larvae that have been hoovered into the vacuum bag from hatching.

The second stage of treatment is to apply an adult insecticide to the dog. Traditionally, this would be in the form of a collar or a spray, but more recent innovations include digestible insecticides that poison the fleas when they ingest the dog's blood. Alternatively, there are drops that, when placed on the back of the animal's neck, spread throughout the fur and skin to kill adult fleas.

> **DID YOU KNOW?**
> Never mix flea control products without first consulting your veterinary surgeon. Some products can become toxic when combined with others and can cause serious or fatal consequences.

TICKS AND MITES

Though not as common as fleas, ticks and mites are found all over the tropical and temperate world. They don't bite, like fleas; they harpoon. They dig their sharp proboscis (nose) into the dog's skin and drink the blood. Their only food and drink is dog's blood. Dogs can get Lyme disease, Rocky Mountain spotted fever (normally found in the US only), paralysis and many other diseases from ticks and mites. They may live where fleas are

An uncommon dog tick of the genus *Ixode.* Magnified 10x.

A brown dog tick, *Rhipicephalus sanguineus*, is an uncommon but annoying tick found on dogs.

The head of a dog tick, *Dermacentor variabilis*, enlarged and coloured for effect.

found and they like to hide in cracks or seams in walls wherever dogs live. They are controlled the same way fleas are controlled.

The dog tick, *Dermacentor variabilis*, may well be the most common dog tick in many geographical areas, especially those areas where the climate is hot and humid.

Most dog ticks have life

Human lice look like dog lice; the two are closely related.

expectancies of a week to six months, depending upon climatic conditions. They can neither jump nor fly, but they can crawl slowly and can range up to 5 metres (16 feet) to reach a sleeping or unsuspecting dog.

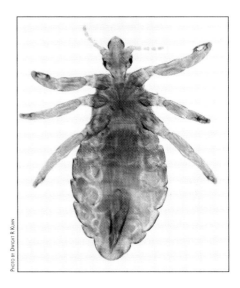

PHOTO BY DWIGHT R KUHN

BEWARE THE DEER TICK

The great outdoors may be fun for your dog, but it also is a home to dangerous ticks. Deer ticks carry a bacterium known as *Borrelia burgdorferi* and are most active in the autumn and spring. When infections are caught early, penicillin and tetracycline are effective antibiotics, but if left untreated the bacteria may cause neurological, kidney and cardiac problems as well as long-term trouble with walking and painful joints.

MANGE

Mites cause a skin irritation called mange. Some are contagious, like *Cheyletiella*, ear mites, scabies and chiggers. Mites that cause ear-mite infestations are usually controlled with Lindane, which can only be

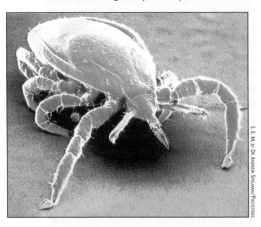

S. E. M. BY DR ANDREW SPIELMAN/PHOTOTAKE

Opposite page:
The dog tick, *Dermacentor variabilis*, is probably the most common tick found on dogs. Look at the strength in its eight legs! No wonder it's hard to detach them.

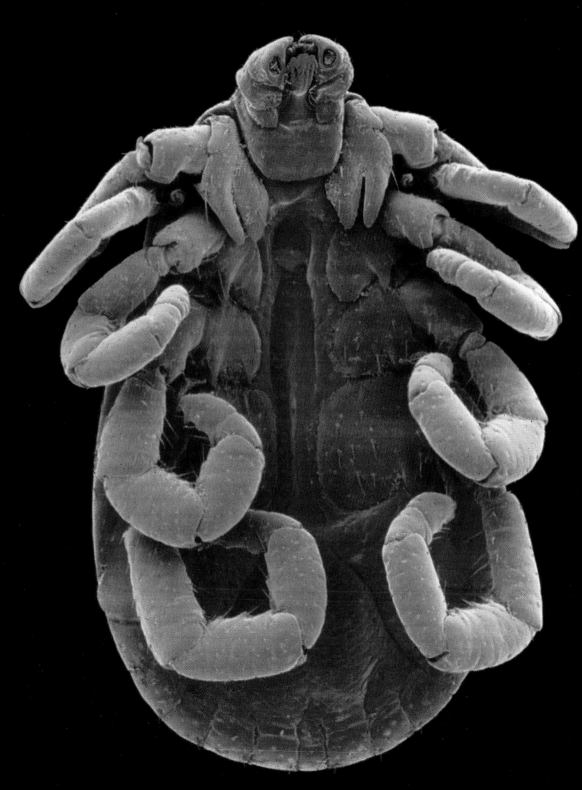

administered by a vet, followed by Tresaderm at home.

It is essential that your dog be treated for mange as quickly as possible because some forms of mange are transmissible to people.

INTERNAL PARASITES

Most animals—fishes, birds and mammals, including dogs and humans—have worms and other parasites that live inside their bodies. According to Dr Herbert R Axelrod, the fish pathologist, there are two kinds of parasites: dumb and smart. The smart parasites live in peaceful cooperation with their hosts (symbiosis), while the dumb parasites kill their hosts.

The common roundworm, Ascaris lumbricoides.

Most of the worm infections are relatively easy to control. If they are not controlled, they weaken the host dog to the point that other medical problems occur, but they are not dumb parasites.

ROUNDWORMS

The roundworms that infect dogs are scientifically known as

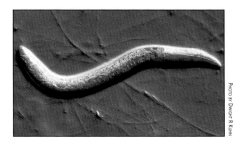

PHOTO BY DWIGHT R KUHN

The mange mite, Psoroptes bovis.

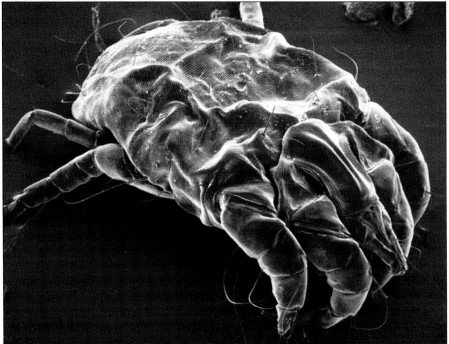

PHOTO BY JAMES HAYDEN-YOAV/PHOTOTAKE

PHOTO BY CAROLINA BIOLOGICAL SUPPLY/PHOTOTAKE

Toxocara canis. They live in the dog's intestines. The worms shed eggs continually. It has been estimated that a dog produces about 150 grammes of faeces every day. Each gramme of faeces averages 10,000–12,000 eggs of roundworms. There are no

ROUNDWORMS

Average-size dogs can pass 1,360,000 roundworm eggs every day. For example, if there were only 1 million dogs in the world, the world would be saturated with 1,300 metric tonnes of dog faeces. These faeces would contain 15,000,000,000 roundworm eggs.

Up to 31% of home gardens and children's play boxes in the US contain roundworm eggs.

Flushing dog's faeces down the toilet is not a safe practice because the usual sewage treatments do not destroy roundworm eggs.

Infected puppies start shedding roundworm eggs at 3 weeks of age. They can be infected by their mother's milk.

DEWORMING

Ridding your puppy of worms is *very important* because certain worms that puppies carry, such as tapeworms and roundworms, can infect humans.

Breeders initiate deworming programmes at or about four weeks of age. The routine is repeated every two or three weeks until the puppy is three months old. The breeder from whom you obtained your puppy should provide you with the complete details of the deworming programme.

Your veterinary surgeon can prescribe and monitor the programme of deworming for you. The usual programme is treating the puppy every 15–20 days until the puppy is positively worm-free. It is advised that you only treat your puppy with drugs that are recommended professionally.

known areas in which dogs roam that do not contain roundworm eggs. The greatest danger of roundworms is that they infect people too! It is wise to have your dog tested regularly for roundworms.

Pigs also have roundworm infections that can be passed to humans and dogs. The typical roundworm parasite is called *Ascaris lumbricoides.*

Left: The roundworm *Rhabditis.* Right: Male and female hookworms. *Ancylostoma caninum* are uncommonly found in pet or show dogs in Britain.

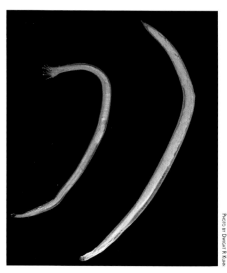

PHOTO BY DWIGHT R. KUHN

PHOTO BY DWIGHT R. KUHN

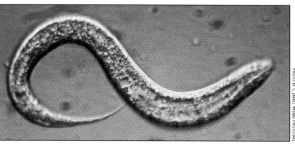

PHOTO BY C. JAMES WEBB/PHOTOTAKE

The infective stage of the hookworm larva.

HOOKWORMS

The worm *Ancylostoma caninum* is commonly called the dog hookworm. It is also dangerous to humans and cats. It has teeth by which it attaches itself to the intestines of the dog. It changes the site of its attachment about six times a day and the dog loses blood from each detachment, possibly causing iron-deficiency anaemia. Hookworms are easily purged from the dog with many medications. Milbemycin oxime, which also serves as a heartworm preventative in Collies, can be used for this purpose.

In Britain the 'temperate climate' hookworm (*Uncinaria stenocephala*) is rarely found in pet or show dogs, but can occur in hunting packs, racing Greyhounds and sheepdogs because the worms can be prevalent wherever dogs are exercised regularly on grassland.

TAPEWORMS

There are many species of tapeworm. They are carried by fleas! The dog eats the flea and starts the tapeworm cycle. Humans can also be infected with tapeworms, so don't eat fleas! Fleas are so small that your dog could pass them onto your hands, your plate or your food and thus make it possible for you to ingest a flea that is carrying tapeworm eggs.

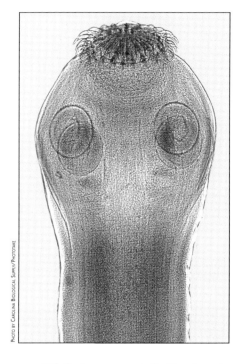

TAPEWORMS

Humans, rats, squirrels, foxes, coyotes, wolves, and domestic dogs are all susceptible to tapeworm infection. Except in humans, tapeworms are usually not a fatal infection. Infected individuals can harbour a thousand parasitic worms.

Tapeworms have two sexes—male and female (many other worms have only one sex—male and female in the same worm).

If dogs eat infected rats or mice, they get the tapeworm disease. One month after attaching to a dog's intestine, the worm starts shedding eggs. These eggs are infective immediately. Infective eggs can live for a few months without a host animal.

The head and rostellum (the round prominence on the scolex) of a tapeworm, which infects dogs and humans.

While tapeworm infection is not life-threatening in dogs (smart parasite!), it can be the cause of a very serious liver disease for humans. About 50 percent of the humans infected with *Echinococcus multilocularis*, a type of tapeworm that causes alveolar hydatis, perish.

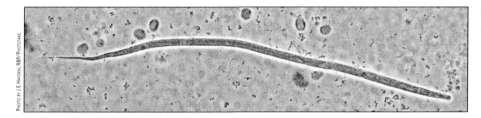

Heartworm, *Dirofilaria immitis*.

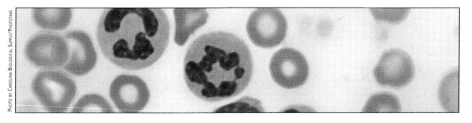

Magnified heartworm larvae, *Dirofilaria immitis*.

HEARTWORMS

Heartworms are thin, extended worms up to 30 cms (12 ins) long, which live in a dog's heart and the major blood vessels surrounding it. Dogs may have up to 200 worms. Symptoms may be loss of energy, loss of appetite, coughing, the development of a pot belly and anaemia.

Heartworms are transmitted by mosquitoes. The mosquito drinks the blood of an infected dog and takes in larvae with the blood. The larvae, called microfilaria, develop within the body of the mosquito and are passed on to the next dog bitten after the larvae mature. It takes two to three weeks for the larvae to develop to the infective stage within the body of the mosquito. Dogs should be treated at about six weeks of age, and maintained on a prophylactic dose given monthly.

Blood testing for heartworms is not necessarily indicative of how seriously your dog is infected. This is a dangerous disease. Although heartworm is a problem for dogs in America, Australia, Asia and Central Europe, dogs in the United Kingdom are not currently affected by heartworm.

The heart of a dog infected with canine heartworm, *Dirofilaria immitis*.

PHOTO BY JAMES E HAYDEN, RPB/PHOTOTAKE

First Aid at a Glance

Burns
Place the affected area under cool water; use ice if only a small area is burnt.

Bee/Insect bites
Apply ice to relieve swelling; antihistamine dosed properly.

Animal bites
Clean any bleeding area; apply pressure until bleeding subsides; go to the vet.

Spider bites
Use cold compress and a pressurised pack to inhibit venom's spreading.

Antifreeze poisoning
Induce vomiting with hydrogen peroxide. Seek *immediate* veterinary help!

Fish hooks
Removal best handled by vet; hook must be cut in order to remove.

Snake bites
Pack ice around bite; contact vet quickly; identify snake for proper antivenin.

Car accident
Move dog from roadway with blanket; seek veterinary aid.

Shock
Calm the dog, keep him warm; seek immediate veterinary help.

Nosebleed
Apply cold compress to the nose; apply pressure to any visible abrasion.

Bleeding
Apply pressure above the area; treat wound by applying a cotton pack.

Heat stroke
Submerge dog in cold bath; cool down with fresh air and water; go to the vet.

Frostbite/Hypothermia
Warm the dog with a warm bath, electric blankets or hot water bottles.

Abrasions
Clean the wound and wash out thoroughly with fresh water; apply antiseptic.

 Remember: an injured dog may attempt to bite a helping hand from fear and confusion. Always muzzle the dog before trying to offer assistance.

HOMEOPATHY:
an alternative to conventional medicine

'Less is Most'

Using this principle, the strength of a homeopathic remedy is measured by the number of serial dilutions that were undertaken to create it. The greater the number of serial dilutions, the greater the strength of the homeopathic remedy. The potency of a remedy that has been made by making a dilution of 1 part in 100 parts (or 1/100) is 1ċ or 1cH. If this remedy is subjected to a series of further dilutions, each one being 1/100, a more dilute and stronger remedy is produced. If the remedy is diluted in this way six times, it is called 6c or 6cH. A dilution of 6c is 1 part in 1,000,000,000,000. In general, higher potencies in more frequent doses are better for acute symptoms and lower potencies in more infrequent doses are more useful for chronic, long-standing problems.

CURING OUR DOGS NATURALLY

Holistic medicine means treating the whole animal as a unique, perfect living being. Generally, holistic treatments do not suppress the symptoms that the body naturally produces, as do most medications prescribed by conventional doctors and vets. Holistic methods seek to cure disease by regaining balance and harmony in the patient's environment. Some of these methods include use of nutritional therapy, herbs, flower essences, aromatherapy, acupuncture, massage, chiropractic and, of course, the most popular holistic approach, homeopathy.

Homeopathy is a theory or system of treating illness with small doses of substances which, if administered in larger quantities, would produce the symptoms that the patient already has. This approach is often described as 'like cures like.' Although modern veterinary medicine is geared toward the 'quick fix,' homeopathy relies on the belief that, given the time, the body is able to heal itself and return to its natural, healthy state.

Choosing a remedy to cure a problem in our dogs is the difficult part of homeopathy. Consult with your veterinary surgeon for a professional diagnosis of your dog's symptoms. Often these symptoms

require immediate conventional care. If your vet is willing, and knowledgeable, you may attempt a homeopathic remedy. Be aware that cortisone prevents homeopathic remedies from working. There are hundreds of possibilities and combinations to cure many problems in dogs, from basic physical problems such as excessive moulting, fleas or other parasites, unattractive doggy odour, bad breath, upset tummy, obesity, dry, oily or dull coat, diarrhoea, ear problems or eye discharge (including tears and dry or mucousy matter), to behavioural abnormalities, such as fear of loud noises, habitual licking, poor appetite, excessive barking and various phobias. From alumina to zincum metallicum, the remedies span the planet and the imagination…from flowers and weeds to chemicals, insect droppings, diesel smoke and volcanic ash.

Using 'Like to Treat Like'

Unlike conventional medicines that suppress symptoms, homeopathic remedies treat illnesses with small doses of substances that, if administered in larger quantities, would produce the symptoms that the patient already has. While the same homeopathic remedy can be used to treat different symptoms in different dogs, here are some interesting remedies and their uses.

Apis Mellifica
(made from honey bee venom) can be used for allergies or to reduce swelling that occurs in acutely infected kidneys.

Diesel Smoke
can be used to help control travel sickness.

Calcarea Fluorica
(made from calcium fluoride, which helps harden bone structure) can be useful in treating hard lumps in tissues.

Natrum Muriaticum
(made from common salt, sodium chloride) is useful in treating thin, thirsty dogs.

Nitricum Acidum
(made from nitric acid) is used for symptoms you would expect to see from contact with acids, such as lesions, especially where the skin joins the linings of body orifices or openings such as the lips and nostrils.

Symphytum
(made from the herb Knitbone, *Symphytum officinale*) is used to encourage bones to heal.

Urtica Urens
(made from the common stinging nettle) is used in treating painful, irritating rashes.

HOMEOPATHIC REMEDIES FOR YOUR DOG

Symptom/Ailment	Possible Remedy
ALLERGIES	Apis Mellifica 30c, Astacus Fluviatilis 6c, Pulsatilla 30c, Urtica Urens 6c
ALOPECIA	Alumina 30c, Lycopodium 30c, Sepia 30c, Thallium 6c
ANAL GLANDS (BLOCKED)	Hepar Sulphuris Calcareum 30c, Sanicula 6c, Silicea 6c
ARTHRITIS	Rhus Toxicodendron 6c, Bryonia Alba 6c
CATARACT	Calcarea Carbonica 6c, Conium Maculatum 6c, Phosphorus 30c, Silicea 30c
CONSTIPATION	Alumina 6c, Carbo Vegetabilis 30c, Graphites 6c, Nitricum Acidum 30c, Silicea 6c
COUGHING	Aconitum Napellus 6c, Belladonna 30c, Hyoscyamus Niger 30c, Phosphorus 30c
DIARRHOEA	Arsenicum Album 30c, Aconitum Napellus 6c, Chamomilla 30c, Mercurius Corrosivus 30c
DRY EYE	Zincum Metallicum 30c
EAR PROBLEMS	Aconitum Napellus 30c, Belladonna 30c, Hepar Sulphuris 30c, Tellurium 30c, Psorinum 200c
EYE PROBLEMS	Borax 6c, Aconitum Napellus 30c, Graphites 6c, Staphysagria 6c, Thuja Occidentalis 30c
GLAUCOMA	Aconitum Napellus 30c, Apis Mellifica 6c, Phosphorus 30c
HEAT STROKE	Belladonna 30c, Gelsemium Sempervirens 30c, Sulphur 30c
HICCOUGHS	Cinchona Deficinalis 6c
HIP DYSPLASIA	Colocynthis 6c, Rhus Toxicodendron 6c, Bryonia Alba 6c
INCONTINENCE	Argentum Nitricum 6c, Causticum 30c, Conium Maculatum 30c, Pulsatilla 30c, Sepia 30c
INSECT BITES	Apis Mellifica 30c, Cantharis 30c, Hypericum Perforatum 6c, Urtica Urens 30c
ITCHING	Alumina 30c, Arsenicum Album 30c, Carbo Vegetabilis 30c, Hypericum Perforatum 6c, Mezerium 6c, Sulphur 30c
KENNEL COUGH	Drosera 6c, Ipecacuanha 30c
MASTITIS	Apis Mellifica 30c, Belladonna 30c, Urtica Urens 1m
PATELLAR LUXATION	Gelsemium Sempervirens 6c, Rhus Toxicodendron 6c
PENIS PROBLEMS	Aconitum Napellus 30c, Hepar Sulphuris Calcareum 30c, Pulsatilla 30c, Thuja Occidentalis 6c
PUPPY TEETHING	Calcarea Carbonica 6c, Chamomilla 6c, Phytolacca 6c
TRAVEL SICKNESS	Cocculus 6c, Petroleum 6c

Recognising a Sick Dog

Unlike colicky babies and cranky children, our canine charges cannot tell us when they are feeling ill. Therefore, there are a number of signs that owners can identify to know that their dogs are not feeling well.

Take note for physical manifestations such as:

- unusual, bad odour, including bad breath
- excessive moulting
- wax in the ears, chronic ear irritation
- oily, flaky, dull haircoat
- mucous, tearing or similar discharge in the eyes
- fleas or mites
- mucous in stool, diarrhoea
- sensitivity to petting or handling
- licking at paws, scratching face, etc.

Keep an eye out for behavioural changes as well including:

- lethargy, idleness
- lack of patience or general irritability
- lack of appetite, digestive problems
- phobias (fear of people, loud noises, etc.)
- strange behaviour, suspicion, fear
- coprophagia
- more frequent barking
- whimpering, crying

Get Well Soon

You don't need a DVR or a BVMA to provide good TLC to your sick or recovering dog, but you do need to pay attention to some details that normally wouldn't bother him. The following tips will aid Fido's recovery and get him back on his paws again:

- Keep his space free of irritating smells, like heavy perfumes and air fresheners.
- Rest is the best medicine! Avoid harsh lighting that will prevent your dog from sleeping. Shade him from bright sunlight during the day and dim the lights in the evening.
- Keep the noise level down. Animals are more sensitive to sound when they are sick.

- Be attentive to any necessary temperature adjustments. A dog with a fever needs a cool room and cold liquids. A bitch that is whelping or recovering from surgery will be more comfortable in a warm room, consuming warm liquids and food.
- You wouldn't send a sick child back to school early, so don't rush your dog back into a full routine until he seems absolutely ready.

Curly Coats are long-lived dogs who remain fairly active for the first decade of their lives.

The term *old* is a qualitative term. For dogs, as well as for their masters, old is relative. Certainly we can all distinguish between a puppy Curly Coated Retriever and an adult Curly Coated Retriever—there are the obvious physical traits, such as size, appearance and facial expressions, and personality traits. Puppies and young dogs like to play with children. Children's natural exuberance is a good match for the seemingly endless energy of young dogs. They like to run, jump, chase and retrieve. When dogs grow older and cease their interaction with children, they are often thought of as being too old to keep pace with the kids. On the other hand, if a Curly Coated Retriever is only exposed to older people or quieter lifestyles, his

Older dogs, referred to as seniors or veterans, slow down in mind and body. Greying on the muzzle is the classic sign of the 'golden years.'

life will normally be less active and the decrease in his activity level as he ages will not be as obvious.

If people live to be 100 years old, dogs live to be 20 years old. While this might seem like a good rule of thumb, it is very inaccurate. When trying to compare dog years to human years, you cannot make a generalisation about all dogs. You can make the generalisation that 10 to 12 years is a good lifespan for a Curly Coated Retriever. Curlies generally are considered physically mature at around three-and-a-half years of age, but can reproduce much earlier. So approximately the first three years of a dog's life are like seven times that of comparable humans. That means a 3-year-old dog is like a 21-year-old human. As the curve of comparison shows, there is no hard and fast rule for comparing dog and human ages. Small breeds tend to live longer than large breeds, some breeds' adolescent periods last longer than others' and some breeds experience rapid periods of growth. The comparison is made even more difficult, for, likewise, not all humans age at the same rate...and human females tend to live longer than human males.

WHAT TO LOOK FOR IN SENIORS

Most veterinary surgeons and behaviourists use the seven- or eight-year mark as the time to consider a Curly Coated Retriever a 'senior.' The term 'senior' does not imply that the dog is geriatric and has begun to fail in mind and body. Ageing is essentially a slowing process. Humans readily admit that they feel a difference in their activity level from age 20 to 30, and then from 30 to 40, etc. By treating the seven- or eight-year-old Curly as a senior, owners are able to implement certain therapeutic and preventative medical strategies with the help of their veterinary surgeons. A

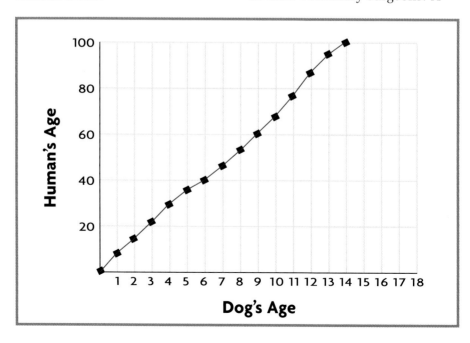

CDS: COGNITIVE DYSFUNCTION SYNDROME
'OLD-DOG SYNDROME'

There are many ways to evaluate old-dog syndrome. Veterinary surgeons have defined CDS (cognitive dysfunction syndrome) as the gradual deterioration of cognitive abilities. These are indicated by changes in the dog's behaviour. When a dog changes its routine response, and maladies have been eliminated as the cause of these behavioural changes, then CDS is the usual diagnosis.

More than half the dogs over eight years old suffer from some form of CDS. The older the dog, the more chance it has of suffering from CDS. In humans, doctors often dismiss the CDS behavioural changes as part of 'winding down.'

There are four major signs of CDS: the dog has frequent toilet accidents inside the home, sleeps much more or much less than normal, acts confused and fails to respond to social stimuli.

SYMPTOMS OF CDS

FREQUENT TOILET ACCIDENTS
- *Urinates in the house.*
- *Defecates in the house.*
- *Doesn't signal that he wants to go out.*

SLEEP PATTERNS
- *Moves much more slowly.*
- *Sleeps more than normal during the day.*
- *Sleeps less during the night.*

CONFUSION
- *Goes outside and just stands there.*
- *Appears confused with a faraway look in his eyes.*
- *Hides more often.*
- *Doesn't recognise friends.*
- *Doesn't come when called.*
- *Walks around listlessly and without a destination.*

FAILS TO RESPOND TO SOCIAL STIMULI
- *Comes to people less frequently, whether called or not.*
- *Doesn't tolerate petting for more than a short time.*
- *Doesn't come to the door when you return home.*

senior-care programme should include at least two veterinary visits per year and screening sessions to determine the dog's health status, as well as nutritional counselling. Veterinary surgeons determine the senior dog's health status through a blood smear for a complete blood count, serum chemistry profile with electrolytes, urinalysis, blood pressure check, electrocardiogram, ocular tonometry (pressure on the eyeball) and dental prophylaxis.

Such an extensive programme for senior dogs is well advised before owners start to see the obvious physical signs of ageing, such as slower and inhibited movement, greying, increased sleep/nap periods and disinterest in play and other activity. This preventative programme promises a longer, healthier life for the ageing dog. Among the physical problems common in ageing dogs are the loss of sight and hearing, arthritis, kidney and liver failure, diabetes mellitus, heart disease and Cushing's disease (a hormonal disease).

In addition to the physical manifestations discussed, there are some behavioural changes and problems related to ageing dogs. Dogs suffering from hearing or vision loss, dental discomfort or arthritis can become aggressive. Likewise, the near-deaf and/or visually impaired dog may be startled more easily and react in an unexpectedly aggressive manner. Seniors suffering from senility can become more impatient and irritable. Housesoiling accidents are associated with loss of mobility, kidney problems and loss of sphincter control as well as plaque accumulation, physiological brain changes and reactions to medications. Older dogs, just like young puppies, suffer from separation anxiety, which can lead to excessive barking, whining, housesoiling and destructive behaviour. Seniors may become fearful of everyday sounds, such as vacuum cleaners, heaters, thunder and passing traffic. Some dogs have difficulty sleeping, due to discomfort, the need for frequent toilet visits and the like.

Owners should avoid spoiling the older dog with too many fatty treats. Obesity is a common problem in older dogs and subtracts years from their lives. Keep the senior dog as trim as possible, since excessive weight puts additional stress on the body's vital organs. Some breeders recommend supplementing the diet with foods high in fibre and lower in calories. Adding fresh vegetables and marrow broth to the senior's diet makes a tasty, low-calorie, low-fat supplement. Vets also offer speciality diets for senior dogs that are worth exploring.

Your dog, as he nears his twilight years, needs your patience and good care more than ever. Never punish an older dog for an accident or abnormal behaviour. For all the years of love, protection and companionship that your dog has provided, he deserves special attention and courtesies. The older dog may need to relieve himself at 3 a.m. because he can no longer hold it for eight hours. Older dogs may not be able to remain crated for more than two or three hours. It may be time to give up a sofa or chair to your old friend. Although he may not seem as enthusiastic about your attention and petting, he does appreciate the considerations you offer as he gets older.

Your Curly Coated Retriever does not understand why his world is slowing down. Owners must make their dogs' transition into their golden years as pleasant and rewarding as possible.

WHAT TO DO WHEN THE TIME COMES

You are never fully prepared to make a rational decision about putting your dog to sleep. It is very obvious that you love your Curly or you would not be

SENIOR SIGNS

An old dog starts to show one or more of the following symptoms:

- The hair on the face and paws starts to turn grey. The colour breakdown usually starts around the eyes and mouth.
- Sleep patterns are deeper and longer, and the old dog is harder to awaken.
- Food intake diminishes.
- Responses to calls, whistles and other signals are ignored more and more.
- Eye contact does not evoke tail wagging (assuming it once did).

reading this book. Putting a beloved dog to sleep is extremely difficult. It is a decision that must be made with your veterinary surgeon. You are usually forced to make the decision when your dog experiences one or more life-threatening symptoms that have become serious enough for you to seek medical (veterinary) help.

If the prognosis of the malady indicates that the end is near and that your beloved pet will only continue to suffer and experience no enjoyment for the balance of its life, then euthanasia is the right choice.

WHAT IS EUTHANASIA?

Euthanasia derives from the Greek, meaning *good death*. In other words, it means the planned, painless killing of a dog suffering from a painful, incurable condition, or who is so aged that it cannot walk, see, eat or control its excretory functions. Euthanasia is usually accomplished by injection with an overdose of anaesthesia or a barbiturate. Aside from the prick of the needle, the experience is usually painless.

MAKING THE DECISION

The decision to euthanise your dog is never easy. The days during which the dog becomes ill and the end occurs can be

> **EUTHANASIA**
> Euthanasia must be performed by a licensed veterinary surgeon. There also may be societies for the prevention of cruelty to animals in your area. They often offer this service upon a vet's recommendation.

unusually stressful for you. If this is your first experience with the death of a loved one, you may need the comfort dictated by your religious beliefs. If you are the head of the family and have children, you should have involved them in the decision of putting your

> **COPING WITH LOSS**
> When your dog dies, you may be as upset as when a human companion passes away. You are losing your protector, your baby, your confidante and your best friend. Many people experience not only grief but also feelings of guilt and doubt as to whether they did all that they could for their pet. Allow yourself to grieve and mourn, and seek help from friends and support groups. You may also wish to consult books and websites that deal with this topic.

Curly Coated Retriever to sleep. Usually your dog can be maintained on drugs for a few days in order to give you ample time to make a decision. During this time, talking with members of your family or with people who have lived through the same experience can ease the burden of your inevitable decision.

Pet cemeteries usually have accommodations for a dog's ashes after cremation.

THE FINAL RESTING PLACE

Dogs can have some of the same privileges as humans. The remains of your beloved dog can be buried in a pet cemetery, which is generally expensive. Dogs who have died at home can be buried in your garden in a place suitably marked with some stone or newly planted tree or bush. Alternatively, your dog can be cremated individually and the ashes returned to you. A less expensive option is mass cremation, although, of course, the ashes cannot then be returned. Vets can usually arrange the cremation on your behalf. The cost of these options should always be discussed frankly and openly with your veterinary surgeon. In Britain, if your dog has died at the surgery, the vet legally cannot allow you to take your dog's body home.

GETTING ANOTHER DOG?

The grief of losing your beloved dog will be as lasting as the grief of losing a human friend or relative. In most cases, if your dog died of old age (if there is such a thing), it had slowed down considerably. Do you want a new Curly puppy to replace it? Or are you better off finding a more mature Curly Coated Retriever, say two to three years of age, which will usually be house-trained and will have an already developed personality. In this case, you can find out if you like each other after a few hours of being together.

The decision is, of course, your own. Do you want another Curly Coated Retriever or perhaps a different breed so as to avoid comparison with your beloved friend? Most people usually buy the same breed because they know (and love) the characteristics of that breed. Then, too, they often know people who have the same breed and perhaps they are lucky enough that one of their friends expects a litter soon. What could be better?

Separation anxiety concerns dog owners today, and many behaviourists are studying the effects of it on the lives of our dogs.

As a Curly Coated Retriever owner, you have selected your dog so that you and your loved ones can have a companion, a protector, a friend and a four-legged family member. You invest time, money and effort to care for and train the family's new charge. Of course, this chosen canine behaves perfectly! Well, perfectly like a *dog*.

Puppies and adults alike can suffer from separation anxiety. Always be sensitive to the psychological needs of your Curly.

THINK LIKE A DOG

Dogs do not think like humans, nor do humans think like dogs, though we try. Unfortunately, a dog is incapable of compre-hending how humans think, so the responsibility falls on the owner to adopt a proper canine mindset. Dogs cannot rationalise, and dogs exist in the present moment. Many dog owners make the mistake in training of thinking that they can reprimand their dog for something he did a while ago. Basically, you cannot even reprimand a dog for something he did 20 seconds ago! Either catch him in the act or forget it! It is a waste of your and your dog's time—in his mind, you are reprimanding him for whatever he is doing at that moment.

The following behavioural problems represent some which Curly owners most commonly encounter. Every dog is unique and every situation is unique. No author could purport to solve your Curly Coated Retriever's problems simply by reading a script. Here we outline some basic 'dogspeak' so that owners' chances of solving behavioural problems are increased. Discuss bad habits with your veterinary surgeon and he/she can recommend a behavioural specialist to consult in appropriate cases. Since behavioural abnormalities are the main reason for owners' abandoning their pets, we hope that you will make a valiant effort to solve your Curly Coated Retriever's problems. Patience and understanding are virtues that must dwell in every pet-loving household.

SEPARATION ANXIETY

Recognised by behaviourists as the most common form of stress for dogs, separation anxiety can also lead to destructive behaviours in your dog. It's more than your Curly Coated Retriever's howling his displeasure at your leaving the house and his being left alone. This is a normal reaction, no different from the child who cries as his mother leaves him on the first day at school. Separation anxiety is more serious. In fact, if you are constantly with your dog, he will come to expect you with him all of the time, making it even more traumatic for him when you are not there. Obviously, you enjoy spending time with your dog, and he thrives on your love and

attention. However, it should not become a dependent relationship in which he is heartbroken without you. This broken heart can also bring on destructive behaviour as well as loss of appetite, depression and lack of interest in play and interaction. Canine behaviourists have been spending much time and energy to help owners better understand the significance of this stressful condition.

One thing you can do to minimise separation anxiety is to make your entrances and exits as low-key as possible. Do not give your dog a long drawn-out goodbye, and do not overly lavish him with hugs and kisses when you return. This is giving in to the attention that he craves, and it will only make him miss it more when you are away. Another thing you can try is to give your dog a treat when you leave; this will not only keep him occupied and keep his mind off the fact that you have just left, but it will also help him associate your leaving with a pleasant experience.

You may have to accustom your dog to being left alone at intervals. Of course, when your dog starts whimpering as you approach the door, your first instinct will be to run to him and comfort him, but do not do it! Really—eventually he will adjust to your absence. His anxiety stems from being placed in an unfamiliar situation; by familiarising him with being alone, he will learn that he will survive. That is not to say you should purposely leave your dog home alone, but the dog needs to know that, while he can depend on you for his care, you do not have to be by his side 24 hours a day. Some behaviourists recommend tiring the dog out before you leave home—take him for a good long walk or engage in a game of fetch in the garden.

When the dog is alone in the house, he should be placed in his crate—another distinct advantage to crate training your dog. The crate should be placed in his familiar happy family area, where he normally sleeps and already feels comfortable, thereby making him feel more at ease when he is alone. Be sure to give the dog a special chew toy to enjoy while he settles into his crate.

AGGRESSION

Although aggression seldom occurs in the Curly Coated

Retriever, this is a problem that concerns all responsible dog owners. Aggression can be a very big problem in dogs, and, when not controlled, always becomes dangerous. An aggressive dog, no matter the size, may lunge at, bite or even attack a person or another dog. Aggressive behaviour is not to be tolerated. It is more than just inappropriate behaviour; it is painful for a family to watch their dog become unpredictable in his behaviour to the point where they are afraid of him. While not all aggressive behaviour is dangerous, growling, baring teeth, etc., can be frightening. It is important to ascertain why the dog is acting in this manner. Aggression is a display of dominance, and the dog should not have the dominant role in its pack, which is, in this case, your family.

Curlies are generally friendly dogs that thrive on the company of other dogs. Aggression is rarely a problem in this gregarious and easygoing breed.

AGGRESSIVE BEHAVIOUR

Dog aggression is a serious problem. NEVER give an aggressive dog to someone else. The dog will usually be more aggressive in a new situation where his leadership is unchallenged and unquestioned (in his mind).

It is important not to challenge an aggressive dog, as this could provoke an attack. Observe your Curly Coated Retriever's body language. Does he make direct eye contact and stare? Does he try to make himself as large as possible: ears pricked, chest out, tail erect? Height and size signify authority in a dog pack—being taller or 'above' another dog literally means that he is 'above' in social status. These body signals tell you that your Curly thinks he is in charge, a problem that needs to be addressed. An aggressive dog is unpredictable; you never know when he is going to strike and what he is going to do. You cannot understand why a dog that is playful one minute is growling the next.

Fear is a common cause of aggression in dogs. Perhaps your Curly had a negative experience as a puppy, which causes him to be fearful when he encounters a similar situation as an adult. The dog may act aggressively in order to protect himself from whatever is making him afraid. It is not always easy to determine what is making your dog fearful, but if you can isolate what brings out the fear reaction, you can help the dog get over it. Supervise your Curly Coated Retriever's interactions with people and other dogs, and praise the dog when it goes well. If he starts to act aggressively in a situation, correct him and remove him from the situation. Do not let people approach the dog and start petting him without your express permission. That way, you can have the dog sit to accept petting, and praise him when he behaves properly. You are focusing on praise and on modifying his behaviour by rewarding him when he acts appropriately. By being gentle and by supervising his interactions, you are showing him that there is no need to be afraid or defensive.

SEXUAL BEHAVIOUR
Dogs exhibit certain sexual behaviours that may have influenced your choice of male or female when you first purchased your Curly Coated Retriever. To a certain extent, spaying/neutering will eliminate these behaviours, but if you are purchasing a dog that you wish to show, you should be aware of what you will have to deal with throughout the dog's life.

Female dogs usually have two oestruses per year, with each season lasting about three weeks. These are the only times in which a female dog will mate, and she usually will not allow this until the second week of the cycle, although this varies from bitch to bitch. If not bred during the heat cycle, it is not uncommon for a bitch to experience a false

HOT TAMALE

Some trainers recommend deterrents, such as hot pepper, a bitter spice or a product designed for this purpose, to discourage the dog from chewing unwanted objects. Test these products to see which works best before investing in large quantities.

pregnancy, in which her mammary glands swell and she exhibits maternal tendencies toward toys or other objects.

With male dogs, owners must aware that whole dogs (dogs who are not neutered) have the natural inclination to mark their territory. Males mark their territory by spraying small amounts of urine as they lift their legs in a macho ritual. Marking can occur both outdoors in the garden and around the neighbourhood as well as indoors on furniture legs, curtains and the sofa. Such behaviour can be very frustrating for the owner; early training is strongly urged before the 'urge' strikes your dog. Neutering the male at an appropriate early age can solve this problem before it becomes a habit.

Other problems associated with males are wandering and mounting. Both of these habits, of course, belong to the unneutered dog, whose sexual drive leads him away from home in search of the bitch in heat. Males will mount females in heat, as well as any other dog, male or female, that happens to catch their fancy. Other possible mounting partners include his owner, the furniture, guests to the home and strangers on the street. Discourage such behaviour early on.

Owners must further recognise that mounting is not merely a sexual expression but also one of dominance, often seen in bitches as well. Be consistent and be persistent, and you will find that you can 'move mounters.'

CHEWING

The national canine pastime is chewing! Every dog loves to sink his 'canines' into a tasty bone, but sometimes that bone is in his owner's hand! Dogs need to chew, to massage their gums, to make their new teeth feel better and to exercise their jaws. This is a natural behaviour that is deeply embedded in all things canine. Our role as owners is not to stop the dog's chewing, but rather to redirect it to positive, chew-worthy objects. Be an informed owner and purchase proper chew toys, like strong nylon bones, that will not splinter. Be sure that the objects are safe and durable, since your dog's safety is at risk. Again, the owner is responsible for ensuring a dog-proof environment.

The best answer is prevention: that is, put your shoes, handbags and other tasty objects in their proper places (out of the reach of the growing canine mouth). Direct puppies to their toys whenever you see them 'tasting' the furniture legs or the leg of your trousers. Make a loud noise to attract the pup's attention and immediately escort him to his chew toy and engage him with the toy for at least four minutes, praising and encouraging him all the while.

JUMPING UP

Jumping up is a dog's friendly way of saying hello! Some dog owners do not mind when their dog jumps up. The problem arises when guests come to the house and the dog greets them in the same manner—whether they like it or not! However friendly the greeting may be, the chances are that your visitors will not appreciate your dog's enthusiasm. The dog will not be able to distinguish upon whom he can jump and whom he cannot. Therefore, it is probably best to discourage this behaviour entirely.

Pick a command such as 'Off' (avoid using 'Down' since you will use that for the dog to lie down) and tell him 'Off' when he jumps up. Place him on the ground on all fours and have him sit, praising him the whole time.

Always lavish him with praise and petting when he is in the sit position. In this way, you can give him a warm affectionate greeting, let him know that you are as excited to see him as he is to see you and instil good manners at the same time!

DIGGING

Digging, which is seen as a destructive behaviour to humans, is actually quite a natural behaviour in dogs. Although terriers (the 'earth dogs') are most associated with the digging, any dog's desire to dig can be irrepressible and most frustrating to his owners. When digging occurs in your garden, it is actually a normal behaviour redirected into something the dog can do in his everyday life. In the wild, a dog would be actively seeking food, making his own shelter, etc. He would be using his paws in a purposeful manner for his survival. Since you provide him with food and shelter, he has no need to use his paws for these purposes, and so the energy that he would be using may manifest itself in the form of little holes all over your garden and flower beds.

Perhaps your dog is digging as a reaction to boredom—it is somewhat similar to someone eating a whole bag of crisps in front of the TV—because they are there and there is nothing better to do! Basically, the answer is to provide the dog with adequate play and exercise so that his mind and paws are occupied, and so that he feels as if he is doing something useful.

Of course, digging is easiest to control if it is stopped as soon as possible, but it is often hard to catch a dog in the act. If your dog is a compulsive digger and is not easily distracted by other activities, you can designate an area on your property where he is allowed to dig. If you catch him digging in an off-limits area of the garden, immediately bring him to the approved area and praise him for digging there. Keep a close eye on him so that you can catch him in the act— that is the only way to make him understand what is permitted and what is not. If you take him to a hole he dug an hour ago and tell him 'No,' he will understand that you are not fond of holes, or

dirt or flowers. If you catch him while he is stifle-deep in your tulips, that is when he will get your message.

BARKING

Dogs cannot talk—oh, what they would say if they could! Instead, barking is a dog's way of 'talking.' It can be somewhat frustrating because it is not always easy to tell what a dog means by his bark—is he excited, happy, frightened or angry? Whatever it is that the dog is trying to say, he should not be punished for barking. It is only when the barking becomes excessive, and when the excessive barking becomes a bad habit, that the behaviour needs to be modified.

Fortunately, Curly Coated Retrievers are not as vocal as

most other dogs. They tend to be discriminating, barking mostly at strangers or unfamiliar things, or sounding a warning when they deem necessary. Excessive habitual barking, however, is a problem that should be corrected early on. As your Curly Coated Retriever grows up, you will be able to tell when his barking is purposeful and when it is for no reason. You will become able to distinguish your dog's different barks and their meanings. For example, the bark when someone comes to the door will be different from the bark when he is excited to see you. It is similar to a person's tone of voice, except that the dog has to rely totally on tone of voice because he does not have the benefit of using words. An incessant barker will be evident at an early age.

There are some things that encourage a dog to bark. For example, if your dog barks non-stop for a few minutes and you give him a treat to quieten him, he believes that you are rewarding him for barking. He will associate barking with getting a treat and will keep doing it until he is rewarded. On the other hand, if you give him a command such as 'Quiet' and praise him after he has stopped barking for a few seconds, he will get the idea that being 'quiet' is what you want him to do.

FOOD STEALING

Is your dog devising ways of stealing food from your coffee table or kitchen counter? If so, you must answer the following questions: Is your Curly Coated Retriever hungry, or is he 'constantly famished' like many dogs seem to be? Face it, some dogs are more food-motivated than others. They are totally obsessed by the smell of food and can only think of their next meal. Food stealing is terrific fun and always yields a great reward—FOOD, glorious food.

Your goal as an owner, therefore, is to be sensible about where food is placed in the home and to reprimand your dog whenever he is caught in the act of stealing. But remember, only reprimand your dog if you actually see him stealing, not later when the crime is discovered; that will be of no use at all and will only serve to confuse him.

BEGGING

Just like food stealing, begging is a favourite pastime of hungry puppies! It achieves that same lovely result—FOOD! Dogs quickly learn that their owners keep the 'good food' for themselves, and that we humans do not dine on dried food alone. Begging is a conditioned response related to a specific stimulus, time and place. The sounds of the kitchen, cans and bottles opening, crinkling bags, the smell of food in preparation, etc., will excite the dog, and soon the paws will be in the air!

Here is the solution to stopping this behaviour: Never give in to a beggar! You are rewarding the dog for sitting pretty, jumping up, whining and rubbing his nose into you by giving him food. By ignoring the dog, you will (eventually) force the behaviour into extinction. Note that the behaviour is likely to get worse before it disappears, so be sure there are not any 'softies' in the family who will give in to little 'Oliver' every time he whimpers, 'More, please.'

COPROPHAGIA

Faeces eating is, to humans, one of the most disgusting behaviours that their dogs could engage in, yet, to dogs, it is perfectly normal. It is hard for us to understand why a dog would want to eat his own faeces. He could be seeking certain nutrients that are missing from his diet, he could be just plain hungry or he could be attracted by the pleasing (to a dog) scent. While coprophagia most often refers to the dog's eating his own faeces, a dog may just as likely eat that of another animal if he comes across it. Vets have found that diets with low levels of

digestibility, containing relatively low levels of fibre and high levels of starch, increase coprophagia. Therefore, high-fibre diets may decrease the likelihood of dogs' eating faeces. Both the consistency of the stool (how firm it feels in the dog's mouth) and the presence of undigested nutrients increase the likelihood. Dogs often find the stool of cats and horses more palatable than that of other dogs. Once the dog develops diarrhoea from faeces eating, he will likely stop this distasteful habit.

To discourage this behaviour, first make sure that the food you are feeding your dog is nutrition-ally complete and that he is getting enough food. If changes in his diet do not seem to work, and no medical cause can be found, you will have to modify the behaviour through environ-mental control before it becomes a habit. The best way to prevent your dog from eating his stool is to make it unavailable—clean up after he eliminates and remove any stool from the garden. If it is not there, he cannot eat it.

Reprimanding for stool eating rarely impresses the dog. Vets recommend distracting the dog while he is in the act of stool eating. Coprophagia is seen most frequently in pups 6 to 12 months of age, and usually disappears around the dog's first birthday.

INDEX

Page numbers in **boldface** indicate illustrations.

My Curly Coated Retriever

PUT YOUR PUPPY'S FIRST PICTURE HERE

Dog's Name _____

Date _____ Photographer _____